At Issue

| DNA Databases

Other Books in the At Issue Series:

At Issue

|DNA Databases

Stefan Kiesbye, Book Editor

GREENHAVEN PRESS
A part of Gale, Cengage Learning

Detroit • New York • San Francisco • New Haven, Conn • Waterville, Maine • London

Elizabeth Des Chenes, *Managing Editor*

For more information, contact:
Greenhaven Press
27500 Drake Rd.
Farmington Hills, MI 48331-3535
Or you can visit our Internet site at www.gale.cengage.com

For product information and technology assistance, contact us at

Gale Customer Support, 1-800-877-4253
For permission to use material from this text or product, submit all requests online at www.cengage.com/permissions

Further permissions questions can be e-mailed to permissionrequest@cengage.com

Articles in Greenhaven Press anthologies are often edited for length to meet page requirements. In addition, original titles of these works are changed to clearly present the main thesis and to explicitly indicate the author's opinion. Every effort is made to ensure that Greenhaven Press accurately reflects the original intent of the authors. Every effort has been made to trace the owners of copyrighted material.

Cover image © Images.com/Corbis.

LIBRARY OF CONGRESS CATALOGING-IN-PUBLICATION DATA

DNA Databases / Stefan Kiesbye, book editor.
    p. cm. -- (At issue) Summary: "DNA Databases: Society Will Benefit from Sharing Information in DNA Databases; Biometric Identification and DNA Databases Are Dangerous to the Public; DNA Databases Help in the Fight Against Crime; Gaps in DNA Databases Prevent Police from Solving Crimes; State DNA Databases Help Solve Crimes; Fighting Crime with DNA Samples Comes With Great Risks; DNA Privacy Violations Are a Serious Problem; DNA Databases Harm Children and Crime Victims; Police Violate Citizens' Rights to Obtain DNA Samples; DNA Databases Help Find the Missing and Identify Human Remains; Familial DNA Searches Might Harm Innocent People; DNA Databases Can Help Determine a Person's Identity; DNA Databases Can Help in Fight Against Animal Cruelty"-- Provided by publisher.
    Includes bibliographical references and index.
    ISBN 978-0-7377-5890-0 (hardback) -- ISBN 978-0-7377-5891-7 (paperback)
    1. Criminal investigation--Juvenile literature. 2. Criminals--Identification-- Juvenile literature. 3. DNA data banks--Juvenile literature. 4. DNA fingerprinting--Juvenile literature. I. Kiesbye, Stefan.
    HV8073.8.D64 2011
    614'.12--dc23

    2011018406

Printed in the United States of America
1 2 3 4 5 6 7 15 14 13 12 11

Contents

Introduction

Since DNA typing (or profiling) was introduced to crime scene investigations in the mid-1980s, it has often been treated like the Holy Grail of forensics; a match between DNA collected at a crime scene and the DNA of a suspect is considered by many to be a failsafe method of establishing guilt. As Michael Bobelian writes in the *Washington Monthly*, "When analyzing DNA, scientists ideally focus on thirteen markers, known as loci. The odds of finding two people who share all thirteen is roughly on par with those of being hit by an asteroid—about one in a quadrillion in many cases."[1]

Since its introduction, DNA evidence has been used to find and convict criminals. Yet it has also become a tool to re-open cold cases and look for suspects many years, and sometimes decades, after a murder was committed—when evidence containing DNA had been collected at the crime scene, but could not be investigated at the time. Several criminals have been caught through old DNA evidence, and many imprisoned people have been exonerated because their DNA did not match the samples. It seems only logical, then, that the FBI's Combined DNA Index System (CODIS) and the National DNA Index System (NDIS) would be an ideal extension of DNA forensics. And by 2007, over 5 million offender samples had been collected, allowing law enforcement to scan forensic profiles and search for matches.

Yet while the successes of DNA forensics have been spectacular, DNA databases come with their own set of risks. Bobelian reports on the 1972 San Francisco rape and murder of Diana Sylvester, a twenty-two-year-old nurse. The case was not solved, but in 2003 the San Francisco Police Department re-opened the case, finding a sperm sample that had been taken from Sylvester's mouth after her murder. Bobelian ex-

1. Michael Bobelian, "DNA's Dirty Little Secret," *Washington Monthly*, March/April 2010.

plains that "the deteriorated sample contained less than half the DNA markers that are normally used to link a suspect to a crime."

However, the police ran the profile through the California DNA database and found a match, subsequently arresting 72-year-old John Puckett. Not only was the sample in bad condition and containing fewer than the necessary count of markers, it was also a "mixed sample", containing DNA from the victim and the perpetrator, which makes it much more difficult to analyze. Puckett went on trial and was convicted without any other evidence linking him to the crime. His appearance did not fit the witness description, and his fingerprints were not found in Sylvester's apartment. The jury was told that the DNA profile had the rarity of "one in 1.1 million," however, and this number had a huge impact on the trial's outcome. Yet the number, Bobelian writes, is misleading. It only applies "when DNA material is used to link a crime directly to a suspect identified through eyewitness testimony or other evidence." When suspects are found by running samples through databases, "the chances of accidentally hitting on the wrong person are orders of magnitude higher." He argues that "when you take a DNA profile that has a rarity of one in a million and run it through a database that contains a million people . . . chances are you'll get a coincidental match." Based on that fact,

> the two leading scientific bodies that have studied the issue—the National Research Council and the FBI's DNA advisory board—have recommended that law enforcement and prosecutors calculate the probability of a coincidental match differently in cold-hit cases. In particular, they recommend multiplying the FBI's rarity statistic by the number of profiles in the database, to arrive at a figure known as the Database Match Probability. When this formula is applied to Puckett's case (where a profile with a rarity of one in 1.1

million was run through a database of 338,000 offenders) the chances of a coincidental match climb to one in three.

British reporters Henry Porter and Afua Hirsch have similar objections to the use of large DNA databases, saying in a 2009 article in *The Guardian* that the British national databases (NDNAD) "is now so large that it is mathematically predicted an innocent person will be matched to a crime they did not commit." Citing scientist Brian Costello, they contend that the problem goes far beyond a merely mathematical problem. "'Two factors will increase the probability of adventitious [incorrect] matches: firstly, the condition of crime scene samples may lead to incomplete profiles; and secondly, individuals who are related are more likely to share the same profile than unrelated individuals.'"[2]

Concerns, however, are raised not only about the value of databases, but also about its maintenance. Simon Ford, the principal of Lexigen Science and Law Consultants, Inc., in San Francisco, and an expert in DNA technology, writes in an article at Bioforensics.com, that "the Philadelphia City Crime Laboratory recently admitted that it had accidentally switched the reference samples of the defendant and victim in a rape case." He also cites the case of "Josiah Sutton, a 16 year old from Houston [who] was falsely convicted of rape in 1996 and sentenced to 25 years in prison based on a misinterpreted DNA test."[3] The mistake was finally corrected, but it raises the question of how many times human error might lead to wrongful convictions.

As the technology advances and states like California grow their databases and allow familial DNA searches that make use of the genetic profiles of many innocent people, the concerns

2. Henry Porter and Afua Hirsch, "The Rising Odds of DNA False Matches," *Liberty Central Blog*, May 25, 2009. www.guardian.co.uk.
3. Simon Ford, "Identifying the Manipulation of DNA Testing Results Through Review of Electronic Data," Forensic Bioinformatics DNA Consulting Services, presented at the Forensic Bioinformatics 6th Annual Conference, August 18, 2007. www.bioforensics.com.

regarding the once infallible-seeming forensic method will grow. The authors of the viewpoints in *At Issue: DNA Databases* explore the impact DNA databases have on our society, their successes and possible applications, whether DNA information can be safeguarded against abuse, and how the databases might be used in the future.

1

Society Will Benefit from Sharing Information in DNA Databases

J. Craig Venter

J. Craig Venter is founder and president of a not-for-profit genomics research organization, and of Synthetic Genomic, which develops and commercializes synthetic genomic advances. He is the author of an autobiography, A Life Decoded.

Because of the tainted history of scientific and government abuse, people are afraid that to share genetic information openly will endanger their integrity and well-being. Yet society has learned from the past, and in order to overcome diseases that still haunt human populations today, sharing DNA in national and global databases is a necessary step. The possible benefits of such databases far outweigh the risk of privacy violations.

As we progress from the first human genome [the entirety of an organism's hereditary information] to sequence hundreds, then thousands and then millions of individual genomes, the value for medicine and humanity will only come from the availability and analysis of comprehensive, public databases containing all these genome sequences along with as complete as possible phenotype [observable characteristic] descriptions of the individuals. All of us will benefit the most by sharing our information with the rest of humanity.

In this world of instant internet, Facebook and Twitter, access to information about seemingly everything and everyone, the idea that we can keep anything completely confidential is becoming as antiquated as the typewriter. Today, in addition to my complete human genome, that of Jim Watson [biochemist who co-discovered the structure of DNA] and some others, medical and genetic information is also readily shared between people on genetic social networking companies who provide gene scans for paying customers. It was my decision to disclose my genome and all that it holds, as it was Jim Watson's and presumably all those others who chat online about their disease risks and ethno-geographic heritage. So while we all have a right to disclose or not to disclose, we have to move on from the equally antiquated notion that genetic information is somehow sacred, to be hidden and protected at all costs. If we ever hope to gain medical value from human genetic information for preventing and treating disease, we have to understand what it can tell us and what it cannot. And most of all we have to stop fearing our DNA.

The public is . . . still back on what they learned from scientists early on: genes determine life outcomes and so you had better not let anyone know the dirty secrets in your genome.

Research Abuses Have Led to Widespread Fear

When we look at our not so distant past it is easy to understand how the idea of the anonymity and protection of research subjects came to pass. The supposed science-based eugenics [the improvement of genetics] movement, the human experiment atrocities of the Nazis and the Tuskegee syphilis research debacle [subjects were not treated for the disease] are just a few examples that prove that we as a society do not have a very good track record on the research front. So naturally when the idea first arose of decoding our human genome, the complete set of genetic material from which all human life springs, it was met largely with fear, including concern of how to adequately protect those involved as DNA donors.

Notions about genetics at the time were based on myth, superstition, misunderstanding, misinformation, misuse, fear, over-interpretation, abuse and overall ignorance propagated by the public, the press and—most surprisingly—even some in the scientific community.

In the 1980s the state of genetic science was not very advanced and the limited tools available led to a very narrow view of human genetics. The only disease-gene associations made then were the rare cases in which changes in single genes in the genetic code could be linked to a disease. Examples include sickle cell anemia, Huntington's disease and cystic fibrosis [a chronic lung disease]. As a result, most began to think that there would be one gene for each human trait and disease, and that we were largely subject to genetic determinism (you are what your genes say you are). An unfortunate slang developed in which people were described as having the "breast cancer gene" or the "cystic fibrosis gene" (instead of the precise way of describing that a mutation in the chloride ion channel associated with cystic fibrosis). In short, people learned that genetics could all be compared with a high-stakes lottery where you either drew the terrible gene that gave you the horrible disease or you got lucky and did not. The notion of applying probability statistics to human genetic outcomes did reach the public.

Today, the science has come a long way since those early days and we now know that there are many genetic changes in many genes associated with genetically inherited diseases like cancer. We also know that genetics is about probabilities and not yes or no answers. However, the public is, for the most part, still back on what they learned from scientists early on: genes determine life outcomes and so you had better not let anyone know the dirty secrets in your genome.

So talk of sequencing the entire human genome created a sort of "perfect storm" of the colliding research ideals of human subject protection and anonymity. The publicly funded, government version of the human genome project went to extremes to use anonymous DNA donors for sequencing, even throwing out millions of dollars of work and data after at least one donor self-identified his contribution to the research.

The Case Against Anonymity

In contrast to the public human genome project, my team at Celera [an institute for disease management] allowed DNA donors to self-identify but Celera itself was bound by confidentiality. Since I was a donor to the Celera project, I thought that one of the best ways to help dissipate the fears of genetic information being misused, or used against me, was to self-disclose my participation as a DNA donor, thereby showing the world that I was not concerned about having my genome on the internet. My colleague at Celera, a Nobel laureate Hamilton Smith, later disclosed that he too was a DNA donor to the Celera genome sequence. My act of self-disclosure and using my own DNA for the first human genome sequence was extensively discussed and criticised by some at the time, including one of the Celera advisory board members, Art Caplan, who likened the genome sequence to the tomb of the Unknown Soldier and wanted it to remain anonymous.

It might all now seem like a quaint historical discussion because of the onslaught of genome announcements and genome companies aiding thousands to share their genetic information with friends, family and the public at large. In 2007 my team and I published my complete diploid genome sequence. This was followed a year later by Jim Watson disclosing his genome identity and releasing his DNA sequence to the internet. Several others have now followed from various parts of the globe. My institute wrestled with the IRB (Institutional review board) issues of sequencing the genome of a known donor as a break from the anonymous past. Following our effort, George Church, a researcher at Harvard, convinced the IRB there to allow full disclosure of multiple individual genomes as part of his project. He and his team have gone even further by including clinical and phenotype information on the internet along with his partial genome sequences.

> *Each and every one of us has a unique genetic code. Understanding our code can have a major impact on our life and health management.*

In the United States the Genetic Information Nondiscrimination Act (GINA) was signed into law in May 2008 after more than a decade of trying to get it through congress. GINA is designed to prohibit health insurers and employers from discriminating against someone on the basis of their genetic information. In order that this protection should be global, other countries should do the same. We are learning more and more all the time about what our genes can tell us about our health and what they still cannot and probably will never tell us.

We have been beginning to see the fruits of our sequencing labours over the last decade but we still have so far to go in understanding our biology. Each and every one or us has a unique genetic code. Understanding our code can have a major impact on our life and health management, particularly in early disease detection and prevention. These advances will only happen with large comprehensive databases of shared information. Your genetic code is important to you, your family members and to the other 6.6 billion of us who are only 1–3% different from you. We will only gain that understanding by sharing our information with the rest of humanity.

2

Biometric Identification and DNA Databases Are Dangerous to the Public

Ethan Jacobs

Ethan Jacobs is a licensed California attorney with a B.A. in political science. He writes on political and social issues for a large number of publications, including BeforeItsNews.com and Old ThinkerNews.com.

In the name of simplification, justice, and defense against terrorists and other criminals, public and private institutions are gathering biometric and DNA information about their citizens or members. Yet the new technologies are far from simple or safe, and could come at the price of civil liberties. Society has to resist new measures to collect genetic data if it wants to stop privacy violations before they can occur. Once DNA and biometric databases have been established, it will be too late to stop abuses built into the governing bureaucracies.

Governments and large corporations are encouraging individuals to identify themselves using biometric data as opposed to traditional card forms of identification, such as drivers' licenses and membership cards. The federal and local governments also have plans to collect DNA samples from people arrested for but not convicted of crimes. The public must take immediate action to stop this assault on privacy rights and prevent the unprecedented implementation of global technocratic tyranny.

Cardless Check-in at Health Clubs

24 Hour Fitness, the world's largest privately owned and operated fitness center chain (by membership) is in the process of implementing its Orwellian "cardless check-in" program:

> 24 Hour Fitness is excited to introduce Cardless Check-In! Cardless Check-In allows members to access our health clubs without a membership card. No more fumbling through you gym bag or purse . . . just scan your finger, enter your 10-digit check-in code and you're on your way. . . . We've partnered with MorphoTrak, a leader in the biometric industry, to develop this convenient new way to check in to our clubs. By scanning your finger, we chart the distance between a few distinct points that are unique to you and come up with an identifying number based on those distances.

24 Hour Fitness has approximately 3 million members, 425 clubs, and 20,000 employees. That equals approximately one percent of the U.S. population (300 million people) that are now being encouraged to produce biometric identification by one health club company alone. It should be noted that for now, members may choose not to enroll, but will need to bring their driver's license or another government or school issued ID each time they check-in.

Providing biometric data, including a fingerprint scan, is an act of submission that is being required by government and private venues more and more.

Importantly, the cardless check-in program has obvious flaws. First, typing in the ten digit code and performing the finger scan takes about twelve times longer than simply scanning the barcode on a membership card. Second, the program weakens human bonding, as now it is no longer necessary to speak to the employee that previously scanned membership cards, assuming their employment has not yet been terminated. Third, a conflict of interest arises if law enforcement requests the biometric data of a member from the health club. Should the health club provide the data or protect the privacy of its member?

It remains to be seen how many 24 Hour Fitness members will voluntarily forfeit their biometric data by leaving their mark on the unblinking scanner. Hopefully the majority will understand that "your fingerprint is a very sensitive piece of your identity. It's not something you can replace if it's compromised."

Global Biometric Plan

Whether intended or not, the 24 Hour Fitness biometric check-in program and others like it assist the Department of Homeland Security in incrementally conditioning the public to accept its Global Biometric Plan. Said plan will further erode personal privacy rights while reducing individuals to a new status of dehumanized biological chattels.

Amusement parks are also requiring biometric identification.

Providing biometric data, including a fingerprint scan, is an act of submission that is being required by government and private venues more and more. To obtain a driver's license, you must submit to a thumb scan. If you refuse, you will not be issued a license, your right to travel will be severely limited, and you will lack a common form of personal identification. In California, a thumb scan is required to obtain a real estate/mortgage broker's license. Beginning February 1, 2011, the Golden State will also require fingerprints to purchase ammunition, a substantial infringement on privacy and the right to bear arms. International travelers that want to skip lines at customs are encouraged to enroll in the Global

Entry Program. After landing, find the Global Entry kiosk, "scan your passport and fingerprints," and be on your way.

Amusement parks are also requiring biometric identification. To utilize an annual pass at SeaWorld, one must participate in the Touch-n-Go finger scan ID verification system. Walt Disney World has also employed a biometric finger scanner at their theme parks.

Blood Sample Gathering

Beyond gathering biometric data on citizens, governments have also been stealing infants' blood samples without parental consent. Of course, this is done under the guise of protecting babies from diseases:

Newborn babies in the United States are routinely screened for a panel of genetic diseases. Since the testing is mandated by the government, it's often done without the parents' consent . . . Now, states mandate that newborns be tested for anywhere between 28 and 54 different conditions, and the DNA samples are stored in state labs for anywhere from three months to indefinitely, depending on the state.

During March of this year [2010], the U.S. House of Representatives approved the Katie Sepich Enhanced DNA Collection Act of 2010 (H.R. 4614) by a vote of 357 to 32. If approved by the Senate, "millions of Americans arrested for but not convicted of crimes will likely have their DNA forcibly extracted and added to a national database." [President Barack] Obama has also endorsed forcing people arrested to submit DNA to a national database." [This bill did not become law in the 111th Congress.]

In Orange County, California, the District Attorney's office has a policy of dropping charges against low-level offenders who agree to submit DNA samples. During 2009, the office nearly quadrupled its DNA database in nine months, with about half of the 15,000 samples being obtained from cases pertaining to minor offences. The Orange County DNA database is separate from the Department of Justice database and those that consent to providing samples commonly do so without legal counsel.

Civil Rights Abuses

Why are governments so interested in obtaining DNA samples from their citizens and what is the long-term agenda? Will the DNA collected be used in experiments or research? This is a vital issue given the fact that "scientists in Israel have demonstrated that it is possible to fabricate DNA evidence, undermining the credibility of what has been considered the gold standard of proof in criminal cases." We should also recall that globalists sponsored the eugenics polices (eliminating the gene pools of those deemed unfit by the state) in the United States that inspired [Adolf] Hitler's Nazis. [According to Edwin Black in "Eugenics and the Nazis—the California Connection," November 9, 2003, at SFGate.com.]

> Hitler and his henchmen victimized an entire continent and exterminated millions in his quest for a so-called Master Race. But the concept of a white, blond-haired, blue-eyed master Nordic race didn't originate with Hitler. The idea was created in the United States, and cultivated in California, decades before Hitler came to power . . . California eugenicists played an important, although little-known, role in the American eugenics movement's campaign for ethnic cleansing. Eugenics would have been so much bizarre parlor talk had it not been for extensive financing by corporate philanthropies, specifically the Carnegie Institution, the Rockefeller Foundation and the Harriman railroad fortune . . . the main solution for eugenicists was the rapid expansion of forced segregation and sterilization, as well as more marriage restrictions. California led the nation, performing nearly all sterilization procedures with little or no due process. In its first 25 years of eugenics legislation, California sterilized 9,782 individuals, mostly women.

In short, history clearly demonstrates that the global elite and governments they control cannot be trusted with the DNA of individuals.

Big Brother and Iris Scanners

In addition to taking our fingerprints and DNA, governments are partnering with private industry (fascism) so that iris scanners can make Leon, Mexico, the "most secure city in the world." Jeff Carter, CDO of Global Rainmakers states:

"In the future, whether it's entering your home, opening your car, entering your workspace, getting a pharmacy prescription refilled, or having your medical records pulled up, everything will come off that unique key that is your iris . . . Every person, place, and thing on this planet will be connected [to the iris system] within the next 10 years . . . If you've been convicted of a crime, in essence, this will act as a digital scarlet letter. If you're a known shoplifter, for example, you won't be able to go into a store without being flagged. For others, boarding a plane will be impossible. . . . When you get masses of people opting-in, opting out does not help. Opting out actually puts more of a flag on you than just being part of the system. We believe everyone will opt-in."

The fraudulent War on Terror is being used to obliterate Fourth Amendment protections against unreasonable search and seizures.

In a follow-up interview, Carter explained: "So we've even worked with three-letter agencies on technology that can capture 30-plus feet away. In certain spaces, eventually, you'll be able to have maybe one sensor the size of a dime, in the ceiling, and it would acquire all of our irises in motion, at a distance, hundreds—probably thousands as computer power continues to increase-at a time."

There is no intention of limiting the use of such technology to small towns in Mexico. "The Homeland Security Department plans to test futuristic iris scan technology that stores digital images of people's eyes in a database and is considered a quicker alternative to fingerprints." As Paul Joseph Watson notes, eventually "Iris records will be held in a database and associated with credit cards and other routine aspects of every day life. The agenda is to replace pin numbers and presentation of photo ID, forcing Americans to submit to high-tech enslavement merely to conduct their day to day activities."

Airport Naked Body Scanners

The fraudulent War on Terror is being used to obliterate Fourth Amendment protections against unreasonable search and seizures. To pass through airport security, without probable cause or even reasonable suspicion of criminal activity, travelers now are required to submit to naked airport body scanners which virtually strip-search and radiate them. Those that opt out of the scanners are groped, and fondled (assault and battery—offensive touching) by TSA [Transportation Security Administration] thugs. Now that travelers and travel industry unions are objecting to naked body scanners on grounds of perversion and radiation, Homeland Security is considering replacing them with body scanners that scan and store biometric data, which in the future could allow citizens to be constantly racked in real time.

People arrested for minor offenses must refuse to provide DNA samples.

Whether the assault on our privacy rights comes from government or the private sector, we must stand strong against it. Individuals must once again respect themselves enough to defend their privacy and constitutional rights. Fortunately, much like the Allied Pilots Union refusing to submit to radio-active naked body scanners, individuals now have an opportunity to opt-out and speak-out against biometric/DNA registries at health clubs, amusement parks, airports and other venues. Respectfully contact companies and government agencies that test these programs; let them know that you disapprove and that your biometric data will never become their property. People arrested for minor offenses must refuse to provide DNA samples. We must resist and exercise peaceful non-compliance against this despotism, as other health clubs and establishments will likely adopt similar biometric identity programs if they think we will accept it. Future generations are counting on us to defend their privacy rights, which can be summarized as the right to be left alone. Remember that courage is contagious; when a brave man or woman takes a stand, the spines of others are often stiffened.

3

DNA Databases Help in the Fight Against Crime

Richard Hurst

Richard Hurst is a senior analyst at Pasco Risk Management, Johannesburg, a global risk consulting company that provides advice and services on challenges in emerging market environments.

Forensic science has been used since the early days of fingerprinting, and the gathering and management of DNA samples is a logical and necessary next step in the effort to fight crime. Because privatizing DNA databases might pose a risk to citizens' safety and legal rights, the government should ensure that violations don't occur. The safety of DNA databases might decide over their success.

In the ongoing fight against the growing and sometimes out of control crime wave that has struck and continues to strike South Africa the use of advanced technology may offer the country a key to being able to address the current huge case backlog and speed up the process of apprehending, prosecuting and convicting repeat offenders.

Forensic science has been used in linking and solving crimes since around 1901 when fingerprinting was used to track offenders. A science which has been used extensively across the world has been that of Deoxyribonucleic acid (DNA) profiling. DNA evidence is generally collected from saliva, blood, semen or perspiration, However, DNA could also be collected from epithelial cells from the skin.

The DNA profiles of suspects may be compared with DNA found at a crime scene while unknown DNA at a crime scene could be scanned against a DNA database of known suspects. The database forms a list of DNA profiles of suspects as well as convicted offenders. A match or a hit may serve to identify the correct or new suspect.

South Africa does indeed have a DNA Database currently but there are plans to extend the reach of the database across the country on a nationwide scale.

DNA databases across the world tend to be motivated by the fact that·

1. A high percentage of criminal tend to be repeat offenders (recidivism) and

2. A small number of criminals are responsible for a number of crimes allowing the database and law enforcement officers to link suspects to numerous crimes.

South Africa does indeed have a DNA Database currently but there are plans to extend the reach of the database across the country on a nationwide scale.

Former South African Police Service (SAPS) Provincial Commissioner DDG, Andre Beukes and Pasco Risk Management Associate says that a DNA Database will be instrumental and crucially important in assisting police officials in being able to swiftly and effectively solve criminal cases.

"It should be regarded as an important tool to aid law enforcement officials in the ongoing fight against crime" added Beukes.

Legislative Challenges

At the heart of the South African development of the envisaged DNA database is the Criminal Law (Forensic Procedures) Amendment Bill of 2009 which when passed has been designed to ensure that every person arrested for alleged offences as well as those convicted will have their DNA profiles loaded onto a national database.

The Bill aims to strengthen the powers and ability of the SAPS in combating crime by expanding their ability to capture DNA finger prints and profiles from samples. In addition it allows for the establishment of a DNA database, which is expected to integrate with the existing SAPS fingerprint database and the digital capture of fingerprint data using advanced biometric technologies.

However, the Bill will also serve to curb police powers, as the acquisition and storage of non intimate DNA samples and profiles may only be carried out by registered medical practitioners.

At the core of this notion is the process and consideration of identity management which would pass constitutional scrutiny ensuring that the fundamental rights of the individual are upheld.

In addition the DNA Database will be integrated with the Department of Home Affairs online system known as Hanis as well as the Department of Transports systems known as e-Natis.

In time its planned that further integration with other government department would take place.

The Costs of DNA Databases

The estimated total cost of the establishment of the DNA Database by the SAPS is expected to be around ZAR[South African rand]9 billion, however the various delays in the implementation of the system and the expected additional cost could see the final budget land up higher than anticipated.

Thus far the budget breakdown has been ZAR3 billion for the upgrade of crime scene and reference sample collection capacity, ZAR2.5 billion for the expansion of the fingerprint database and ZAR2 billion for collection from private laboratories over a period of five years, with the remainder of the funding allocated to the integration of systems.

An issue that has been highlighted has been the possibility of outsourcing the administration of the national DNA Database. The outsourcing would assume the guise of a technology and software related environment which would alleviate the capacity issues currently highlighted by the SAPS.

Technology should be seen by the South African criminal justice system as one of the key enablers to place the forces of good ahead of the curve for once.

However, the Police and Prisons Civil Rights Union (Popcru) have said that they are in favour of the SAPS retaining the capacity as part of their core functions under the SAPS Criminal record and Forensic Science services Division (CR and FSS). The division currently administers and maintains the Automated Finger print Identification Systems (AFIS) which according to Popcru should manage the National DNA Database.

The recent delays in the development and implementation of a DNA Database are reported to have been the interdepartmental integration of services.

In addition the SAPS have come out in favour of delaying the proposed legislation with an eye to developing the capacity in phases.

DNA Database Risks

Technology should be seen by the South African criminal justice system as one of the key enablers to place the forces of good ahead of the curve for once.

"However, the implementation of the DNA Database in South Africa carries a variety of risks the first relates to the custody of evidence and the related knock on effect on the all important chain of evidence," cautioned Beukes.

In terms of the current proposals the SAPS are expected to be the custodians of the DNA Database but the possibility of outsourcing the database is a concept being considered by the South African government. However, should the database become the domain of another privately run entity there is a risk that the chain of evidence may come into question, creating a loophole which will serve to only work against the current crime fighting initiatives.

"The integrity of evidence should not be comprised at all costs," concluded Beukes.

4

Gaps in DNA Databases Prevent Police from Solving Crimes

Associated Press

Founded in 1846 and headquartered in New York, the Associated Press (AP) is a global news network, serving daily newspaper, radio, television, and online customers with coverage in text, photos, graphics, audio, and video. MSNBC.com is a news website containing supplemental content for NBC and MSNBC news programming.

As the case of murder suspect Walter Ellis demonstrates, the current system of gathering DNA samples is flawed. It is too easy for prison inmates, such as Ellis, to tamper with DNA swabs, and the overwhelmed state agencies in charge of growing and maintaining DNA databases cannot effectively prevent abuses. Backlogs stemming from understaffed labs and a glut of DNA samples hinder progress and open doors to confusion and costly mistakes. While DNA databases have the potential to be an effective tool, the reality of the existing systems puts any long-term success in doubt.

During what police say was a 20-year killing spree in Milwaukee, Walter Ellis left his DNA behind all along the way—everywhere but the one place where it might have saved a life.

Ellis should have given a DNA sample to the state crime databank during a prison stint in the early part of this decade, but he had another inmate pose as him, authorities say. As a result, when analysts tried to identify DNA in bodily fluids from one of the slayings back in 2003, no matches turned up.

Investigators didn't connect Ellis to the crimes until this fall [2009], when they seized genetic material from his toothbrush. By then, it was too late for the woman police say was Ellis' seventh and final victim.

Tens of thousands of DNA samples are missing from state databanks across the country because they were never taken or were lost.

"If they would have got his DNA when they were supposed to get it, maybe my cousin would still be here," said Sarah Stokes, whose cousin, 28-year-old prostitute Ouithreaun Stokes, was found beaten and strangled in an abandoned rooming house in 2007.

Many Samples Are Missing

An Associated Press [AP] review found tens of thousands of DNA samples are missing from state databanks across the country because they were never taken or were lost. The missing evidence—combined with big backlogs at the nation's crime labs that result in DNA samples sitting on shelves for years without being analyzed and entered into the databanks—is preventing investigators from cracking untold numbers of cases. And some of those gaps have had tragic consequences.

"If you got missing samples, some of those people are out there raping your wives and abducting and murdering your children this week," said former Charlottesville, Va., police Capt. J.E. Harding, who helped uncover missing samples in that state during a search for a serial rapist.

Confusing Laws Blamed

Crime lab supervisors, state police and prison officials blame the failure to collect samples on new and confusing laws and a lack of coordination among the many different law enforcement agencies and institutions responsible for taking DNA.

"I would just about guarantee you every state has an issue with this," said Lisa Hurst, who tracks DNA convictions for Gordon Thomas Honeywell, an organization that lobbies on public safety and biotechnology issues.

The AP review found 27 states either failed to collect some DNA samples or are unable to say whether they took one from every offender who owes one.

At least 13 states are dealing with more samples than they can handle.

The case against Ellis, who is set to go trial this spring [2010], prompted an audit in Wisconsin that found 12,000 convict samples are missing. The AP review further found that Illinois failed to get DNA from about 50,000 offenders, Colorado from 2,000, and Virginia from about 8,400.

Exactly how many samples are missing across the country is unknown. The National Institute of Justice estimated in 2003 that offenders owed up to 1 million uncollected samples and as many as 300,000 samples may be waiting for processing. The backlog grew to about 450,000 by 2008. The institute had no updated estimate of uncollected samples.

Backlog at Labs

At least 13 states are dealing with more samples than they can handle. Kansas, for example, has nearly 40,000 on its crime lab shelves, waiting for upload.

Police in Columbus, Ohio, say Robert N. Patton Jr. committed 37 rapes over a decade and a half. As with Ellis in Milwaukee, he could have been stopped earlier.

Patton had submitted his DNA in 2001 while behind bars for burglary, but it was not entered into the database until 2004, two days before he climbed through an apartment window and raped Diana Cunningham. Police say he attacked 13 women in all after supplying his DNA.

If Patton's genetic material "had been processed in a timely fashion, he never would have gotten to me or gotten to any of the others," said Cunningham, now 25. "It's scary how many more people are going to be victimized because their attackers aren't going to be caught. And it would be so easy for them to be caught if they could make the matches."

Patton is now serving a 68-year prison sentence.

7.4 Million Samples

State databanks contain hundreds of thousands of samples. The FBI's national database, built with states' uploads, held 7.4 million as of September [2007].

Generally, prison officials collect DNA from inmates as they enter the institution, often by swabbing the prisoner's mouth.

Over the past 15 years, tough-on-crime legislators expanded laws to require DNA from more offenders. First it was sex offenders. Today, 47 states demand DNA from every convicted felon. Twenty-one take it from anyone arrested for homicide or a sex crime, according to Gordon Thomas Honeywell.

Generally, prison officials collect DNA from inmates as they enter the institution, often by swabbing the prisoner's mouth. Local police, sheriff's departments or probation officers are also supposed to take samples. That means a profusion of collection points.

But the laws are so fluid that the agencies responsible for collecting DNA struggle to track which offenders owe samples, authorities say. The New Mexico lab has taken to sending wall charts to sheriff's departments to help them keep things straight.

Wisconsin Gov. Jim Doyle has blamed his state's missing DNA, in part, on confusion over the laws during the early days and no clear idea of who was in charge.

Cross-checking Records

Roughly half the states have some cross-check between their labs and prison systems to ensure everyone who owes a sample has given it, the AP found. For example, Michigan DNA administrators and state prison officials compare information annually. Virginia requires that it be done quarterly. But half the states have no such procedures.

Robyn Quinn, Delaware's DNA database administrator, said she is sure her state is missing DNA, but has no idea how much, citing lack of communication between her office and the Corrections Department.

"The other end is a black hole for me. We have no way of getting into their system to see who is supposed to be collected," she said. "I am waiting for something to hit the fan, if you will."

5

State DNA Databases Help Solve Crimes

P. Solomon Banda

P. Solomon Banda is a contributor to AP Worldstream, a division of the Associated Press.

DNA databases are helping to solve crimes—some of which have been dubbed "cold cases"—and exonerate people charged with crimes they did not commit. Matching the DNA from possible offenders to samples that were taken at the crime scene can help police identify criminals. DNA databases have proven very effective in solving property crimes, especially in Denver, Colorado.

The burglar was undone by his taste for strawberry soda.

RazJohn Smyer, a suspect in a string of Denver-area break-ins, often checked his victims' refrigerators and helped himself to a drink. The soda cans he left behind gave police enough DNA evidence to link him to five burglaries. He is now serving a 20-year sentence.

Jason L. Hanson, 30, is serving a 70-year sentence for the 1997 kidnapping of a child from Box Elder. Pennington County authorities have now accused him of raping another child that same year. If convicted of first-degree rape, he could spend the rest of his life in prison.

Smyer's conviction is just one example of how DNA evidence is increasingly being used to solve everyday property crimes across the U.S. Once reserved mostly for violent cases such as rape and murder, genetic testing is now much cheaper and faster than when the technology was new.

By using DNA, authorities are five times more likely to identify a suspect than with fingerprints alone.

"Regular watchers of 'CSI' may be led to believe that this technology is already being used in this way, but it's really brand-new," said John Roman of the Urban Institute, lead author of a study on the issue. "This really is the start of a revolution in policing."

The evidence can include almost any biological material left at a crime scene: saliva taken from food, skin cells from the steering wheel of a stolen car, drops of blood from a thief who got cut on a window pane.

By using DNA, authorities are five times more likely to identify a suspect than with fingerprints alone. DNA also doubles the number of suspects who are identified, arrested and prosecuted, according to the study, which was funded by the National Institute of Justice.

Burglars identified with DNA evidence in Denver usually plead guilty because prosecutors "have very solid evidence," said Denver District Attorney Mitch Morrissey.

For many years, the high cost of DNA tests and the long wait for results made it difficult for authorities to use the technology in property crimes.

But genetic testing has come a long way since 1989, when investigators needed a blood sample about the size of a half dollar or a seminal fluid stain the size of a dime to perform an accurate analysis, which took about 10 weeks and cost $1,000.

"It was great for the prosecution, but it wasn't good for the investigation," recalled Paul Ferrara, who recently retired as director of Virginia's state crime lab and developed the nation's first DNA databank.

"My only surprise today is that it's been this long in coming."

Analysis on some cases now takes as little as 12 hours and costs only about $50.

In Denver, detectives linked a suspect to five burglaries after he left saliva on a piece of "gold coin" candy.

Police in New York City and Chicago use DNA testing routinely. Other agencies, such as the Los Angeles Police Department, still reserve it for the most serious crimes. Police in Great Britain began using DNA for property crimes in 2001.

In Denver, detectives linked a suspect to five burglaries after he left saliva on a piece of "gold coin" candy. The man, who was on parole when he committed the burglaries, is now serving a 48-year sentence.

Another thief was arrested after detectives found his DNA on a tuna sandwich. In a different case, investigators were even able to extract DNA from part of a lollipop left at a crime scene.

Once genetic material is analyzed, a profile is developed and compared with state databases or entered into the FBI's Combined DNA Index System, which contains 6 million offender profiles and more than 225,000 pieces of evidence awaiting a match.

"We've been able to link DNA to what were totally unsolved, closed cases," said Lt. Kip Lowe of the Topeka Police Department in Kansas. "And when that DNA was submitted, that information funneled back to us and, boom, we identified the suspect."

The National Institute of Justice found that processing a scene for DNA evidence, following up on leads and eventually identifying a suspect adds about $4,502 to the cost of a property crimes investigation.

That expense has paid off in Denver, where the average sentence in property crime cases using DNA evidence jumped to 14 years, compared with 1 1/2 years for those without DNA. Part of the reason: Suspects identified in the DNA database are habitual offenders and can be linked to more than one crime, Morrissey said.

He estimated that Denver saved more than $4.4 million in stolen property and police time between November 2005 and July 2007 by removing repeat offenders from the streets.

Many of the worst offenders commit hundreds of property crimes in a year—sometimes as many as four or five in a single day, Morrissey said.

Los Angeles police Commander Harlan Ward said grant money from the Urban Institute study allowed his department to conduct DNA tests in several cases, including one involving a man who had 35 previous felony arrests. But once the study ended, the department restricted DNA use to violent crimes.

Property crimes such as burglary, theft and auto theft cost Americans an estimated $17.6 billion in 2007, according to the FBI.

"The issue is one of capacity," said Barry Fisher, director of the Los Angeles County Sheriff's Department crime lab and past president of the American Society of Crime Lab Directors.

"The federal government doesn't pay for the bulk of crime labs. That comes from general funds that are approved by city councils, board of commissions, legislatures. We need to be able to answer, 'What is the value in doing this?' We're just now starting to get a hint with these studies."

Some police agencies, including the Chicago Police Department, rely on state and county crime labs to process DNA samples, which can take months. For example, at the Miami-Dade County crime lab, scientists process evidence from at least 35 agencies.

"You can send over a thousand samples, and the property crimes would take less priority (than a violent crime), and rightfully so," said Miami Police Chief John Timoney.

In the Denver suburb of Aurora, Police Chief Dan Oates is considering hiring an analyst to work with the Colorado Bureau of Investigation state crime lab.

"In the end, whether it's cost effective will be irrelevant," Oates said. "Police will demand it. Prosecutors will demand it. Defense attorneys will demand it. Juries will demand it."

6

Fighting Crime with DNA Samples Comes with Great Risks

Liliana Segura

A former writer and editor at AlterNet, where she was in charge of Rights & Liberties and World Special Coverage, Liliana Segura now works as a journalist and editor with a focus on social justice, prisons, and harsh sentencing.

When a new bill forcing convicted felons to provide DNA samples was introduced, it received little negative attention. Yet the success of intended DNA databases is less than assured. The corruptibility of databases looms large, and any rush to create new laws regarding sample-sharing among agencies might make the system vulnerable to abuse. While DNA samples have played a role in exonerating the falsely imprisoned, logistical problems and budgetary constraints can overwhelm forensics labs and law enforcement. Without a proper debate, DNA databases might endanger civil liberties and human rights.

On June 1st [2010], amid talk of teacher layoffs, hospital closings, and MTA [Metropolitan Transportation Authority] cuts, Gov. David Paterson took to a microphone in Manhattan and announced the All Crimes DNA Bill, which he described as "a small investment in dollars, and a huge investment in the security and safety of New York State." The law would force any New Yorker convicted of a crime to pro-

Liliana Segura, "Albany's DNA Expansion: A Foolproof Solution?" *Brooklyn Rail*, July 2010. Copyright © 2010 The Brooklyn Rail. All rights reserved.

vide a DNA sample to authorities, to be recorded in the state DNA database. This would apply to "youthful offenders"—age 16, 17, or 18—and would include such low-level misdemeanors as loitering, graffiti, and shoplifting. Failing to submit a DNA sample would become a Class A misdemeanor, generally punishable by up to one year in jail.

Gov. Paterson characterized the bill as an effort to cut through "a lot of government red tape" and to fix major flaws in the criminal justice system, from unsolved crimes to wrongful convictions. "We have technology and we have data that can help to prevent crimes that are about to be committed, solve crimes that were committed sometime ago, and exonerate people who are falsely accused," he said at his press conference, flanked by D.A.s [District Attorneys] from all five boroughs.

New Databases Receive Little Opposition

If there was any objection to Paterson's proposal from lawmakers or political candidates, no one spoke up. In fact, alternative versions of the DNA expansion were being simultaneously peddled by lawmakers, including a bill from Sen. Jeffrey Klein (D-Bronx) that would require all New Yorkers arrested for a felony to hand over DNA. A bill by Brooklyn Assembly member Joseph Lentol focuses on wrongful convictions and has the support of Sen. Eric Schneiderman (D-Manhattan), who is running for attorney general.

New York would be the first to make it standard practice to create DNA profiles for anyone found guilty of a crime.

Indeed, like so much tough-on-crime legislation, the measure was widely embraced as a moral imperative. Kate Hogan, President of the State District Attorneys Association, called it "simply unconscionable that New York State still neglects to collect DNA from everyone convicted of a penal law crime."

In fact, despite the rhetoric, it shouldn't be surprising: neither does any other state in the country.

"We would be the first state to require DNA from everyone convicted of a penal offense," says John Caher, Director of Public Information of New York's Division of Criminal Services in Albany. Although all 50 states and the federal government have passed laws authorizing DNA testing of convicted felons—and some 21 states require testing of anyone merely arrested for a federal crime—New York would be the first to make it standard practice to create DNA profiles for anyone found guilty of a crime. "We're not following the lead of any other state," says Caher, describing the legislation as "a very, very clean bill that does one very simple thing: It expands the DNA databank."

Success of DNA Databanks Is Doubtful

But this simple idea brings real-life complexities that should give legislators pause. From backlogged DNA samples to falsified forensics reports, the unintended consequences of widespread DNA collection across the country call into question how productive Paterson's "investment" in the safety of New York State will be.

In the 15 years since New York's database was first created, there has never been a comprehensive review of how effective it has actually been in fighting crime.

Two weeks after Paterson's press conference, the New York Civil Liberties Union (NYCLU) released a nine-page document titled "Unanswered Questions about Proposals to Expand the State's DNA Databank," which warned that the All Crimes DNA Act is being advanced "without a single legislative hearing, without a word of public debate, and without a showing of findings or data regarding the proposal."

"It is fair to assume that after a political calculation has been made, there is not much to talk about," the NYCLU statement read. "In this information void, the guiding policy prescription regarding the databank has been reduced to simplistic policy formulation: The more DNA, the better."

The NYCLU cited recent research and data that pose important questions regarding the potential corruptibility of the DNA database—from human error and inefficiency to lack of oversight or accountability. Indeed, while growing the DNA databank is seen by many as a public safety no-brainer, in the 15 years since New York's database was first created, there has never been a comprehensive review of how effective it has actually been in fighting crime.

The same is true of the national DNA database or Combined DNA Index System (CODIS), established by [President] Bill Clinton and expanded under [President George W.] Bush. Bruce Budowle, a former DNA scientist for the FBI who helped design it, has said that "a better accounting of how well CODIS performs is needed," including whether or not "cold hits"—DNA samples taken from a crime scene and matched to a record in the database—are actually leading to prosecutions. Among his questions are whether crime laboratories are "overworked" and whether sufficient resources exist to carry out investigations based on DNA hits.

The eagerness to expand the New York database parallels the rush to establish it in the first place.

For Robert Perry, Legislative Director for the NYCLU, the problem is not even that such questions remain unanswered. It's that they haven't even been asked. "There has not been any serious probing into what we are building," he told me from Albany in late June, as lawmakers and lobbyists scrambled before the start of the summer break.

Databanks Lack Oversight

The eagerness to expand the New York database parallels the rush to establish it in the first place. "When the databank was created, there was no hearing, there was no floor debate. It was created at the staff level and simply voted on as a fait accompli [something that is complete or established]," Perry recalls. At minimum, Perry says, the expansion of New York's DNA database must be accompanied by a system for oversight, ideally in the form of an independent body with sufficient resources and a mandate to do its job. But, he adds, "these things are not looked kindly upon. Every time [legislators] see 'task force' they see expenditure."

Nonetheless, the NYCLU has issued a formal draft proposal to make such oversight either a condition for enactment of the DNA expansion, or as a part of the bill itself. "We're not Luddites [people opposed in principle to technological change] at the ACLU," Perry says. "Under optimum circumstances, DNA can be a valuable forensic tool. What we argue is that circumstances are often not optimal."

If the alarming number of wrongful convictions in New York raises questions about competency and corruption among the same authorities who would be in charge of handling newly expanded DNA collection, no one seems to be making the connection.

There's no question that DNA evidence has played a critical role in freeing the innocent—particularly in New York. This past February, 60-year-old Freddie Peacock from Rochester became the 250th DNA exoneration in the United States, after spending 20 years in prison and an additional 28 years on parole for a rape he did not commit. That month, the Innocence Project reported that New York is the state with the third highest number of DNA exonerations in the country.

Then, in April, another Rochester man, Frank Sterling, was exonerated, 18 years after being convicted of a murder he did not commit. Most recently, on June 21, Douglas Pacyon of Cheektowaga, NY, became the latest DNA exoneree, cleared of a 1984 rape.

The Criminal Justice System Is Flawed

But if the alarming number of wrongful convictions in New York raises questions about competency and corruption among the same authorities who would be in charge of handling newly expanded DNA collection, no one seems to be making the connection.

The NYCLU cites a 2009 report by the State Inspector General that revealed a case of forensic analyst working in a state police crime lab who falsified test results over the course of 15 years. "The analyst had not been properly trained; his superiors not only condoned the fraudulent conduct, but attempted to conceal it." A similar revelation came out in a 2007 report, which "concluded that police department lab analysts had falsified forensics tests and that the NYPD had failed to adequately investigate and report that evidence had been compromised."

Broke and short-staffed, the forensics lab couldn't keep up with its growing number of DNA records.

On the national level, Stanford criminologist William C. Thompson has found "an unexpectedly high" rate of mix-ups and "cross-contamination," which could actually lead to more wrongful convictions by switching an innocent person's DNA with that of a guilty person. Even more troubling: examples of analysts faking results in order to cover up mistakes—perhaps in part because, as the *Chicago Tribune* reported in 2004, "the discovery of even a single flawed analysis" in a given lab "raises the prospect of re-examining hundreds, if not thousands, of cases. In many jurisdictions, the task of re-evaluating that many cases is so daunting that authorities have declined to conduct broad audits, despite evidence that analysts have committed errors or engaged in fraudulent practices."

Logistical Problems Abound

Then there is the problem of backlogs. Legislators might consider the nightmare in Los Angeles last summer, when less than a year after enacting a new policy of testing all rape kits for DNA (instead of just those recommended for testing by investigators), the L.A. Sheriff's Department was forced to announce that it was temporarily suspending DNA testing in sexual assault cases. Broke and short-staffed, the forensics lab couldn't keep up with its growing number of DNA records. The new policy had been established under intense political pressure, but it was "never realistic," one supervisor confessed to the *L.A. Times*.

Beyond practical questions of effectiveness and corruptibility, fundamental civil liberties questions have barely made it into the discussion.

In New York, according to John Caher of Criminal Services, the expanded DNA collection would add roughly 48,000 records to the databank per year. While Caher states that "we don't have a backlog," accelerating DNA collection seems to be a good way to create one. What's more, according to the NYCLU's Robert Perry, "the regulatory scheme that we have [to oversee DNA labs] was put in place in 1994. At that time it was considered visionary. Now it is an anachronism. It simply isn't up to the task of providing the rigor of review and analysis of how these labs are functioning."

Beyond practical questions of effectiveness and corruptibility, fundamental civil liberties questions have barely made it into the discussion. Nor has the fact that, in a state where

77 percent of prisoners are black or Latino, the DNA database will increasingly reflect this bias. "To the extent error and fraud is involved in the use of forensic DNA, the individuals harmed will most often be persons of color," says the NYCLU.

"Familial Searching" Might Violate Civil Rights

Those who claim that only guilty persons will be affected by the DNA expansion aren't quite right, either. Last December, the New York State Commission on Forensic Science voted to authorize police to "investigate the family members of an individual whose DNA does not precisely match crime scene evidence, but is a near match," according to the NYCLU. Called "familial searching," it hinges on the idea that a partial or close match between a DNA sample in a databank and DNA left at a crime scene could mean that a relative was responsible for the crime.

Perry calls familial searching "a profound expansion of the use of forensic DNA," and the forensics commission's policy a "really provocative proposal that's been moving under the radar." In his opinion, the commission is overstepping its authority, but legislators have yet to protest. Although the All Crimes DNA Act does not mention familial searching specifically, such an increase in DNA collection would open the door for many more innocent blood relatives implicated in a criminal investigation.

Despite all these questions, New York lawmakers seem ready to wave the DNA expansion through without blinking an eye. "This is a frenzied place and legislators are preoccupied with not only their own bills, but with a budget that is probably the most challenging in 50 years," says Perry. "By and large, these guys—they are mostly guys—just seem incurious. They just have not thought about these issues."

7

DNA Privacy Violations Are a Serious Problem

Emily Ramshaw

Emily Ramshaw writes about state agencies and social services for the Texas Tribune. *In 2009 she was named Star Reporter of the Year by the Texas Associated Press Managing Editors and the Headliners Foundation of Texas.*

While blood samples have long been taken from newborn babies to check for birth defects and diseases, they were never meant to be used for research by outside labs. Yet in the state of Texas, blood and DNA from infants were routinely sold without parents' consent, violating privacy regulations, opening the doors to unwanted screenings by law enforcement, and potentially abusing the rights of children and their parents. Despite a new effort to inform the public about possible uses of DNA samples, outside labs are not forced to destroy the ones previously obtained, confirming many citizens' fears about DNA databases.

When state health officials were sued last year [2009] for storing infant blood samples without parental consent, they said it was for medical research into birth defects, childhood cancer and environmental toxins. They never said they were turning over hundreds of dried blood samples to the federal government to help build a vast DNA database—a forensics tool designed to identify missing persons and crack cold cases.

A *Texas Tribune* review of nine years' worth of e-mails and internal documents on the Department of State Health

Services' newborn blood screening program reveals the transfer of hundreds of infant blood spots to an Armed Forces lab to build a national and, someday, international mitochondrial DNA (mtDNA) [DNA found in organelles called mitochondria rather than in the cell nucleus] registry. The records, released after the state agreed in December to destroy more than 5 million infant blood spots, also show an effort to limit the public's knowledge of aspects of the newborn blood program, and to manage the debate around it. But the plaintiffs who filed the lawsuit never saw them, because the state settled the case so quickly that it never reached the discovery phase.

Good Intentions

DSHS spokeswoman Carrie Williams says that while the department's general philosophy was to save blood spots for public health research, "we did not have an exclusive policy." She says DSHS participated in the project because officials believed it would help in missing-persons cases—and knew the blood spots could not be linked back to a particular individual. "Our understanding of mtDNA is that it's not used to pinpoint exactly who a person is, but can help determine origins," Williams says. "Our intentions were good ones."

For decades, the state has screened newborns for a variety of birth defects, pricking their heels and collecting five drops of blood on a paper card.

But Jim Harrington, the civil rights attorney who filed the blood spot lawsuit last year on behalf of five Texas parents, believes DSHS meant to deceive the public. When he was negotiating with state officials, he says, he specifically asked what research the blood spots were being used for—and there was no mention of the federal mtDNA project. He says he was stunned by how quickly the state settled the lawsuit. "Sometimes there are slam-dunk cases, but I'd never seen this kind of case settle without discovery," says Harrington, director of the Texas Civil Rights Project. "This explains the mystery of why they gave up so fast."

For decades, the state has screened newborns for a variety of birth defects, pricking their heels and collecting five drops of blood on a paper card. Until 2002, the cards were thrown out after a short storage period. But starting that year, the state health department began storing blood spots indefinitely, for "research into causes of selected diseases." Four years later, DSHS began contracting with Texas A&M University's School of Rural Public Health to warehouse the cards, which were accumulating at a rate of 800,000 a year. State health officials never notified parents of the changes; they didn't need consent for the birth-defect screening, so they didn't ask for it for research purposes. The agency's rationale was that it let parents who asked opt out of the newborn blood screening and de-identified all of the samples before shipping them off.

The State Acted in Secret

Over the last several years, researchers have requested Texas baby blood spots for a variety of medical projects: to study the gene involved in club foot, to inspect the DNA of infants who develop childhood cancer, to examine prenatal lead exposure. Those are the projects state health officials have touted repeatedly before lawmakers and critics. But the least publicized of these research projects is arguably the most interesting. Between 2003 and 2007, the state gave 800 de-identified blood samples to the Armed Forces DNA Identification Laboratory (AFDIL) to help create a national mtDNA database.

MtDNA is extremely valuable in forensics because it's easier to find and extract from human cells than nuclear DNA. In addition to blood, it can be identified in hair, bones, teeth and damaged or degraded biological samples and can be used to identify victims of mass disasters or to solve long-since-cold criminal cases. But it's only as valuable as its sample size.

AFDIL scientists, in conjunction with the research branch of the Justice Department, approached Texas in a $1.9 million effort to expand the country's mtDNA database—part of the President's DNA Initiative launched under George W. Bush. The researchers wanted "anonymous and maternally unrelated" blood samples from Texas Caucasians, African-Americans and Asians—and from Hispanics and Native Americans in particular—to round out their genetic record. The researchers also took samples from prison populations and infant blood screening in other states, including Florida, Minnesota and California. They did not pay Texas for the samples.

Whether Texas officials were concerned about the perception of the project, or simply didn't think it was newsworthy, they never mentioned it.

Eventually, research proposals indicate, federal officials hoped to be able to share this data worldwide, "for international law enforcement and investigation in the context of homeland security and anti-terrorism efforts."

Whether Texas officials were concerned about the perception of the project, or simply didn't think it was newsworthy, they never mentioned it. In presentations, in public reports and in e-mails sent to reporters as recently as last year, state health officials never brought up the federal project—even when they discussed the merits of roughly two dozen medical research projects designed to "unlock the causes of childhood disorders" like autism and diabetes.

In November, when *The Texas Tribune* first filed an open-records request with DSHS to review blood spot records, the agency said the information requested was confidential. Two weeks later, when the lawsuit settlement was formally signed, the *Tribune* asked again, and this time the agency relented. But the box of documents officials turned over hardly referenced the mtDNA project, aside from a single e-mail referencing a "US Department of Justice/National Institute of Justice and the Armed Forces Institute of Pathology/Armed Forces DNA Identification Laboratory." When the *Tribune* pressed health officials about the missing research files, they produced them, saying it was an oversight, and that the documents had been overlooked in their initial search.

Legal Issues Were Ignored

The records the agency initially released paint a portrait of an agency that walked on eggshells around the baby blood spot collection—from 2001, when lawmakers first debated whether to warehouse the cards, through last year, when they passed a law in response to the civil rights lawsuit giving parents better options to opt out.

In 2001, when the Legislature considered a newborn-blood-spot collection bill that state health officials didn't like, they took action. In an e-mail chain, an associate commissioner described how she and another official "planted questions" and "planted a note" with sympathetic lawmakers (former state Reps. Bob Glaze, D-Gilmer, and Glen Maxey, D-Austin) before a public hearing. "I suspect this bill will die . . ." wrote the official, who no longer works for the state. (The bill didn't make it out of committee.) Glaze couldn't be reached for comment. Maxey said he couldn't recall the bill but routinely met with health department staffers to pick their brains about pertinent bills.

E-mails indicate that in 2003, when the agency started to release blood spots for outside research, officials knew they had a parental consent issue on their hands—but tried to avoid it. When a researcher proposed a project, the director of birth defects monitoring wrote that he'd "prefer to not have to go through" the process of getting consent. Another agency official responded that parents "never consented for blood spots to be used for research. . . . On the other hand, I believe [the health department] already uses (deidentified?) blood spots for some research, so that might not be a big deal."

In 2006, when the agency was beginning to store blood spots at Texas A&M, the university asked for permission to put out a press release announcing it. The agency balked. "What do you think of this idea? Makes me a bit nervous," the manager of the birth defects surveillance division wrote in an e-mail to five of his colleagues. Another responded: "This makes me nervous. Genetic privacy is a big ethical issue & even though . . . approval is required for use of the spots in most situations and great care is taken to protect the identity of the spots, a press release would most likely only generate negative publicity." One official asked the university not to do it; the university agreed.

Scientists say baby blood spot research is incredibly valuable, and that the genetic origins of human diseases can be traced through mtDNA samples if there are enough available.

When asked about the e-mails, agency officials said a decision not to send out a press release "isn't an indication of our level of openness." "We don't routinely do news releases about every agency initiative or contract," Williams says, "and obviously this is a sensitive topic." But they acknowledged that staff members are not permitted to "plant" questions with lawmakers. Given that the e-mail exchange happened in 2001, and that the employee no longer works for the agency, Williams says, "there is no way for me to definitively tell if there was any punishment."

An Important Mission Continues

Scientists say baby blood spot research is incredibly valuable, and that the genetic origins of human diseases can be traced through mtDNA samples if there are enough available. They say there are fail-safe methods for stripping identifying information from the samples, so they could never be used for illicit purposes. The problem, some say, is that scientists have used the public's unease with the subject as an excuse not to talk about it. "As scientists, we've failed in teaching people about genetics in the United States," says Dr. Bennett Van Houten, a molecular oncologist at the University of Pittsburgh Cancer Institute who formerly worked at the University of Texas Medical Branch in Galveston. "We need to work harder at that—at teaching them the facts."

Williams says that at the direction of lawmakers last session, parents now receive more information at the hospital about the storage and use of bloodspots and are given a better opportunity to opt out. While the agency is destroying more than 5 million baby blood spots collected before the new legislation took effect, she says, officials are not asking outside researchers—including those at the Armed Forces lab—to return the samples they were given. But they must destroy them when they are done with them.

"The core mission is to screen all babies for life-threatening disorders," Williams says. "We care deeply about this mission, and we have made some changes and are moving forward."

8

DNA Databases Harm Children and Crime Victims

David Pollard

David Pollard studied physics at Oxford and writes about natural science, with a particular focus on its social, psychological and philosophical implications.

DNA profiling has proven many prisoners innocent and has helped to solve cold cases, but unless everybody will be required to submit DNA samples, it's irresponsible and potentially harmful to keep children's DNA, as well as that of people who volunteered theirs for a specific case, in a national database. While police are already imagining ways to predict crime using DNA databases, it seems more urgent to address political and social justice to keep crimes from occurring. Since data security has been weak, children's databases should be abolished.

Together with about 250 others, my profile is on the National DNA Database (NDNAD) in connection with the rape and murder of my partner forty years ago. The police asked that samples should be volunteered during their 1997 re-investigation. Despite the firm assurance that they would be used in this enquiry "for the purposes of elimination only", these profiles remain on the database.

This can't be right. It was a lie that the samples were for the purpose of elimination only. Now the Child Database is under development, and there is no reason whatever to sup-

David Pollard, "DNA Databases Harm Kids—and Victims of Crime," *The First Post*, April 2, 2009. www.thefirstpost.co.uk. Copyright © 2009 The First Post Newsgroup IPR Limited/Felix Dennis. All rights reserved.

pose that the authorities will display any greater scruples about the way in which data is managed and gathered than they have shown with the NDNAD.

A Matter of Trust

If the authorities lie, then why should anyone else choose not to? And why should we trust them with our data? The ND-NAD was at one stage promoted with an emotive question, "Ask the family or friends of any victim if they are in favour of the database, and they will invariably answer, 'Yes'." Well, I for one said, 'No'; but my MP [Member of Parliament] didn't listen to my concerns and nor did others whom I approached.

Being pragmatic, it's clear that a proportion of those who commit crimes aren't entirely sane.

Perhaps I can find some consolation, though: since inventing DNA profiling in the 1980s, Professor Sir Alec Jeffreys has argued consistently—and rightly, as I see it—that the NDNAD will be socially unjust unless everyone is on it; and no-one in government has listened to him either.

Being pragmatic, it's clear that a proportion of those who commit crimes aren't entirely sane. Irrational though it may be, they simply believe they will never get caught. Or, in the heat of the moment, they just don't care about the consequences.

Those who take a more cold-blooded approach will find ways to circumvent DNA tracing. Already, for example, some criminals spread a selection of other people's cigarette ends at the scene of the crime. There are, of course, more effective ways to lay a false trail or hide the evidence.

DNA profiling has, it's true, provided a result in a number of highly publicised cold cases. Future crimes, however, will become more difficult to detect. There is one factor that is by far the most important in solving crime: the co-operation of the general public. Co-operation doesn't mean turning us into a nation of curtain twitchers, snitching at every opportunity, but it does need a certain amount of trust that the system is fair.

If the authorities lie, then why should anyone else choose not to?

Databases Are Not Failsafe

Misuse of the NDNAD has without doubt eroded goodwill towards the police; and announcements by a variety of high-flying politicians that they would be happy to be profiled has done little to restore this loss of trust. When it comes to the child database, it is clear that their progeny's data would be "shielded".

The inclusion of profiles of innocent people and children on the NDNAD, many only tangentially associated with any crime; the deceit in keeping samples volunteered "for the purpose of elimination only"; and the lack of response to the unanimous verdict of the European Court of Human Rights, which found that retention of profiles of innocent people infringes their rights—all these cannot but have eroded the public's trust.

"Don't get involved," rather than being the excuse of a few when the police ask for help, may well become the maxim of many. It is now being said of the DNA database that it doesn't provide a silver bullet solution, though that isn't the story we were being told a year or two ago.

The authorities' new one-click crimestop is, it seems, going to be the children's database. RYOGENS, or Reducing Youth Offending Generic National Solution, as part of the system is called, will collect and combine data from a wide variety of sources—schools, medical records, social services, census data, local council, police etc—and predict which children are likely to become offenders, though this part of the system is now promoted more on the basis of identifying those that are "at risk".

> *Most teachers don't need a database to know which of their pupils has a problem; nor are they short of ideas which would improve education.*

It analyses a selection of factors such as where they live; who their friends are; how stable their family is and how much income it has; how often they have been late for medical or dental appointments; their parents' mental and sexual health, and so forth. This is tackling the problem entirely the wrong way round. If the relevant factors in being able to predict a person's criminality are already well known, then by the same token so too are the causes—the causes that need to be addressed directly, without having to identify anyone through intrusive recording of personal data on a nationwide scale.

And to address the causes rather than to punish the predictable effects in labelled individuals would not incur the undoubted costs of stigmatisation, loss of freedom, privacy and trust, and errors that will inevitably occur if this computerised overseer is brought into being. Most teachers don't need a database to know which of their pupils has a problem; nor are they short of ideas which would improve education.

Databases Cannot Deal with Youth Offenders

Similarly with the police force. It may be over-idealistic to hope that a quiet word or a stern word with a tearaway will instantly reform them; but it makes more sense for the police to be out and about on the street rather than doing computerised paperwork or playing armchair detective. And medical practitioners often have a difficult enough job when dealing with sensitive issues without patients' additional reluctance to explain relevant details for fear that these may be recorded as a damaging database entry that is later used against them.

The argument "if you've done nothing wrong then you have nothing to fear" didn't work with the NDNAD and it doesn't work any better here. Nor does the imposition on generally dedicated public servants of a further layer of meddlesome bureaucracy. Three crucial questions must be asked when personal data is stored, especially when children are involved. 1) Is the system secure? 2) Are those who access and manage the data essentially free from corruption? 3) Is it appropriate to collect and collate the data? The government's record speaks for itself in answer to the first question. Incompetence and bungling are words that spring to mind. As to the second, figures suggest that maybe ten percent of the population has a criminal streak, or that seven percent show psychopathic tendencies.

Misuse of the DNA database has without doubt eroded goodwill towards the police.

Whatever the proportions may be, there's no obvious reason to think they are very much different in the public sector than overall. And though some criminals may indeed have been caught and excluded, others may be undetected. Any system would need to be as immune to those with access to it as it is to the tangible miscreants in the wider community. Clearly a multi-agency nationwide child database, even with monitored access, would fail that test.

Misuse of the DNA database has without doubt eroded goodwill towards the police.

Data Security Cannot Be Guaranteed

To answer the third question: the problem is not just what use will be made of the child database now, it is what might happen in the future. The potential for misuse is one that would overwhelm the aspirations of even the greatest tyrants in history. And don't children have a right to make a mistake without carrying the burden until they are adult—or, indeed, for the rest of their life?

Though the records will supposedly be jettisoned when they become adult, what guarantee is there that this will actually be done? When DNA profiling was introduced, this was to have been on the basis that records of innocent or acquitted people would be removed from the database. There's no guarantee at all of what future use might be made of the children's data. Currently the UK [United Kingdom] is spending billions of pounds each year on database systems.

Appalling is too weak a word to describe the government's record on data security and waste in implementation of computer systems. Surely it would be better to spend less on national databases and more on tackling problems at a local level, and where solutions are already obvious. The children's database should be first to go.

9

Police Violate Citizens' Rights to Obtain DNA Samples

James Slack

James Slack is the Home Affairs Editor of the London Daily Mail.

In order to gather more and more DNA samples for a national database, police in Britain arrest people even if they do not suspect them of having committed a serious crime. The British DNA database costs taxpayers an inordinate amount of money, yet the system appears to be unsafe and to violate civil rights. The British government seems to keep the database running for its own sake, without apparent attempts to safeguard privacy or curb police abuses.

P olice are arresting innocent people in order to get their hands on as many DNA samples as possible, senior Government advisers revealed last night [November 23, 2009].

The Human Genetics Commission [HGC] said the Big Brother tactic was creating a 'spiral of suspicion' among the public.

The panel—which contains some of Britain's leading scientists and academics—said officers should no longer routinely take samples at the point of arresting a suspect.

They also called for all police—including support staff—to place their own DNA on the national database in a show of solidarity with a public being routinely placed under suspicion.

By law, officers are only allowed to make an arrest if they have 'reasonable suspicion' that a person has committed a crime.

But the HGC, which has carried out a lengthy review of the merits of the database, said evidence had emerged of police arresting people purely so they could take their DNA.

Campaigners have long feared officers were carrying out mass sweeps of the population to load their samples on the database, and make future crime fighting easier.

Unwarranted Arrests Are Common

Its chairman, Professor Jonathan Montgomery, said: 'People are arrested in order to retain DNA information that might not have been arrested in other circumstances.'

The claim, which was backed by evidence from a senior police officer, delivers a significant blow to the Government's defence of the database—which contains more than 5.6 million samples.

Campaigners have long feared officers were carrying out mass sweeps of the population to load their samples on the database, and make future crime fighting easier.

The result is one million entirely innocent people having their genetic details logged by the state.

The Commission said one of the consequences of current DNA laws was that young black men are 'very highly over-represented', with more than three quarters of those aged 18–35 on the database.

Professor Montgomery warned this was creating a 'spiral of suspicion' among sections of society.

A retired senior police officer, a superintendent, told the commission: 'It is now the norm to arrest offenders for everything if there is a power to do so.

'It is apparently understood by serving police officers that one of the reasons, if not the reason, for the change in practice is so that the DNA of the offender can be obtained.'

There are no plans to reduce police powers to take samples on arrest.

Officers in England and Wales are entitled to take samples from everyone they arrest for a recordable offence.

Proposals within the Crime and Security Bill—published last week [November 2009]—will for the first time put a time limit, in most cases six years, on how long profiles are stored when the alleged offender is either not charged or later cleared.

But there are no plans to reduce police powers to take samples on arrest.

The Benefit of DNA Databases Is in Doubt

One possibility is to only take DNA when a suspect is charged—making it harder for police to target innocents for their DNA.

In a 110-page report, the commission said more detailed research is required to evaluate how useful the database is in helping to solve crimes, describing current evidence as 'flimsy'.

It accused politicians of using single case studies where the database has secured a conviction instead of carrying out a rigorous evaluation of its scale and function.

Latest Government figures show the costs of running the system—the largest in the world—have risen dramatically, to £4.3 million from £2.1 million in just a year.

Over the past two years, more than 1.17 million new profiles have been added to the database but the number of DNA-related detections fell from a peak of 41,148 in 2006–07 to 31,915 in 2008–09.

LibDem spokesman Chris Huhne said: 'The Government's cavalier attitude to DNA retention has put us in the ridiculous situation where people are being arrested just to have their DNA harvested.

'Ministers make no distinction between innocence and guilt and as a result everyone is treated like a suspect.'

Liberty [Liberal Democrats] warned police were being given a 'perverse incentive' to arrest individuals just to get their details on the database.

Tory home affairs spokesman James Brokenshire said: 'For too long the Government has had a policy of growing the DNA database for the sake of it, regardless of guilt or innocence.'

Tories last night attacked reported Government plans to charge innocent people a £200 fee to apply to have their names removed from the national DNA database.

And they called for England and Wales to follow the Scottish model by not retaining the DNA of such innocents, save in exceptional circumstances. The Government has proposed such DNA should be kept for six years.

Tory security spokesman Baroness Neville-Jones told the Lords: 'If it is the case that making an application for removal is subject to a £200 fee, several individuals will be prevented from making any appeal or indeed getting their names off the database.

'Perhaps the Government is using the right of individuals to appeal to help fill the big public sector deficit.'

10

DNA Databases Help Find the Missing and Identify Human Remains

Michael A. Fuoco

Michael A. Fuoco has been a staff writer at the Pittsburgh Post-Gazette *since 1984. He is part of the enterprise reporting team, and is an adjunct professor of journalism at Pittsburgh's Point Park University.*

With the help of NamUs, a publicly available database, relatives and friends of missing persons can help police solve cold cases. While databases are still incomplete, DNA samples can help identify victims of murder even decades after the crime. DNA samples and databases give new hope to people who are looking for parents, friends, and siblings.

For nearly a decade, the remains of a female homicide victim discovered in Wilkinsburg have been stored in the Allegheny County morgue, awaiting what she had in life but lost in death—an identity.

The mummified remains of another unidentified woman were found in Homestead in 2000; the cause of her death was undetermined. The body of a third woman, the victim of a drug overdose, was discovered in the Allegheny River near the Fox Chapel Yacht Club in 2003.

Those three mysteries are among the 40,000 cases of unidentified human remains that are stored in the offices of the nation's medical examiners and coroners. Just as sobering: on any given day there are as many as 100,000 active missing person cases in the United States.

The Problem of Identifying Human Remains

To deal with what it has termed a national "mass disaster over time," the National Institute of Justice [NIJ] has developed two new databases to more efficiently match information about unidentified remains to missing persons.

By entering characteristics such as sex, race, distinct body features and dental information, anyone can search the Unidentified Decedents Database, where information is entered by medical examiners and coroners.

The National Missing and Unidentified Persons System, known by the acronym "NamUs"—available on the Internet at www.namus.gov—is the first national repository for records about missing persons and unidentified dead people, including both the Unidentified Decedents Database and the Missing Persons Database.

Also unique to the system is the access it grants to the general public, which NIJ views as a valuable asset in helping to solve cases. By entering characteristics such as sex, race, distinct body features and dental information, anyone can search the Unidentified Decedents Database, where information is entered by medical examiners and coroners.

And the Missing Persons Database contains information that, once verified, can be entered by anyone. The site also provides links to state clearinghouses, medical examiners and coroners, victim assistance groups and pertinent legislation.

The unidentified remains database has been online since 2007; the missing persons site has been up since January

[2009]. NIJ is now working on software that would automatically search each database for matches.

Nationally, there are now 1,354 missing person cases in the system. Pennsylvania has 25 open missing person cases in the system—12 men and 13 women.

Those numbers will grow exponentially as more cases are added by law enforcement agencies, clearinghouses and the public, said Richard Mac-Knight, NamUs regional system administrator responsible for Pennsylvania, New York, New Jersey and Washington, D.C.

Cold Cases Are Reexamined

The oldest missing person case listed for Pennsylvania is that of Curtis Eutsey, of Mount Pleasant, who was 18 when he was last known to be alive on Jan. 1, 1992. Today, he would be 35. According to his case listing, "Curtis left his girlfriend's residence with two unknown individuals."

The only other Western Pennsylvania case currently listed is that of Lonnett Jackson, 46, who was last seen on April 11, 2006, "at approximately 11 a.m. at her residence in the vicinity of the 5100 block of Chaplain Way in Hazelwood." Also in the listing: Ms. Jackson has a medical condition and needs medication.

Ed Strimlan, chief forensic investigator for the Allegheny County medical examiner's office, said the county's three cases of unidentified remains have been included for years in other national databases. About six months ago, the office also entered those cases into NamUs.

The results surprised him.

"We got about 10 to 15 calls from multiple states about different possibilities. None of them panned out, but at least we were able to [exclude them]."

Some queries came from law enforcement agencies. Others came from citizens who volunteer their time to groups like the Doe Network, an Internet-based volunteer clearinghouse of missing persons and unidentified bodies. Because the public, including families of the missing and other advocates, has access to NamUs, he said, there is great potential for increased success in identification.

Joni Lapeyrouse, of Pensacola, Fla., couldn't agree more.

In March 1979, at age 30, Ms. Flickinger left for California with a man to get her troubled life together, promising she'd return for her five children, ages 6 to 12. She was never heard from again.

"Allowing average people to get on there is going to take a load off police officers who don't have time to go and search for every cold case," she said. "Lord knows I've done enough searching on the Internet."

Looking for Answers

For years she's been trying to find out what happened to her aunt, former Erie resident Nellie Florence Cornman Flickinger.

In March 1929, at age 30, Ms. Flickinger left for California with a man to get her troubled life together, promising she'd return for her five children, ages 6 to 12. She was never heard from again.

In July 2007, Ms. Lapeyrouse contacted the Doe Network, which the next day reported a possible match with unidentified female skeletal remains discovered in 1982 in a drainage ditch northwest of Sacramento. In addition to hair color, height and age, the biggest match between her aunt and the remains was a metal plate screwed into bones of the right leg.

The remains are now at the University of North Texas Center For Human Identification in Fort Worth, which is seeking to extract DNA from a femur and tooth in hopes of matching it to DNA provided by Ms. Flickinger's relatives.

On Thursday [February 19, 2009], after learning about NamUs and surfing the sites, Ms. Lapeyrouse asked Erie police to help her enter Ms. Flickinger's case into the missing person database.

In the meantime, she searched NamUs's unidentified remains database using her aunt's physical characteristics and found a potential match in Arizona. She contacted the law enforcement agency involved in the case but learned that woman's DNA didn't match anything in another national database, where that of her aunt's relatives also is stored.

Still, NamUs is a godsend because it provides the public with the opportunity to help search for answers to such painful mysteries and does so in an efficient way.

That is the goal, NamUs's Mr. MacKnight said.

"It's very important for the loved ones of missing persons. They can't start the grieving process until they know what happened," he said. "Even if it's years later and the body of their loved one is located, it lets them begin the grieving process."

11

Familial DNA Searches Might Harm Innocent People

Jessica Cerretani

Jessica Cerretani is a writer and editor who covers health, nutrition, green living, and lifestyle topics for a variety of magazines and websites.

Familial searching has led to several convictions in California and Colorado, most famously in the case of the serial killer nicknamed "The Grim Sleeper." Yet while comparing DNA patterns and looking for partial matches—instead of looking for perfect ones, as was the norm—might lead to a few spectacular success stories, the practice of storing the DNA of innocent people in large databases comes at a high risk. Minorities are heavily overrepresented in California's database, raising issues of racism and racial profiling, and it also raises the specter of police harassing criminals' innocent family members. If familial searches do not want to lose credibility, legal issues and logistics have to be worked out before DNA databases start sharing information nationally.

In the end, it was a slice of pizza that sealed his fate: In a scene straight from CSI [the television series *Crime Scene Investigation*], a police officer disguised as a waiter retrieved the partly eaten crust and tableware abandoned by the suspect on a restaurant table. Soon, tests confirmed that the DNA in saliva on the pizza matched evidence from a crime scene. That suspect, Lonnie Franklin Jr., is accused of being the serial killer nicknamed the "Grim Sleeper," who left a trail of at least 10 victims in Los Angeles over a 25-year span. He was arrested in July [2010] and has pleaded not guilty to murder charges.

Familial DNA Searching

Italian food may have been Franklin's downfall, but a less common, and more controversial, forensic technique led police to the suspect in the first place. Known as familial DNA searching, it scours existing DNA databases for partial matches that suggest an unidentified suspect may be a close relative of someone in the database. In the case of the Grim Sleeper, such a search pinpointed DNA that partially matched DNA found at one of the killer's crime scenes, though it belonged to a man too young to have committed some of the murders. Further investigation revealed a probable suspect: that young man's father, Lonnie Franklin Jr. His capture marks the first time that the technique—currently employed only by California and Colorado—has been used in the United States to help solve a homicide case.

No two people, save identical twins, have the exact same DNA sequence, but first-degree relatives like parents, children, and siblings share similar genetic patterns.

"For those of us who support the judicious use of familial DNA searching in the US, this case is the Holy Grail we've been searching for," says Frederick Bieber, a medical geneticist at Brigham and Women's Hospital and associate professor of pathology at Harvard Medical School. Bieber and other proponents of familial searching hope the apparent success of the Grim Sleeper case will motivate more states, including Massachusetts, to create a policy that gives investigators permission to implement the technique. But whether Massachusetts will eventually do so is uncertain. The Massachusetts State Police crime lab has a new director, Guy Vallaro, a forensic toxicologist, and he says there are no immediate plans to implement the type of DNA database searching that California and Colorado are using. "California has done a very thorough job of ensuring that they have all the quality measures in place for familial searching," he says. "But that takes a lot of time and money."

Looking for Genetic Patterns

Familial DNA searching and a related technique called case-specific partial matching draw on basic genetic truths: We receive half of our DNA from our mother and half from our father. No two people, save identical twins, have the exact same DNA sequence, but first-degree relatives like parents, children, and siblings share similar genetic patterns. When compared in the lab, DNA samples belonging to a father and son, for example, aren't an exact match, but the similarities signal a close familial relationship. . . .

It's this concept of kinship analysis that informs paternity tests and can help identify victims of crimes and natural disasters. It was, in fact, Bieber's work with New York investigators after the terrorist attacks of September 11, 2001, that accelerated his thinking on the potential uses for kinship analysis. Now one of this country's most vocal champions of familial DNA searching, Bieber was part of a panel of scientists who consulted on how DNA samples from 9/11 victims' families were used to help identify remains when no DNA sample from the missing person (from a toothbrush, for example) was available. "It made sense," he says, "that we should make more effective use of kinship analysis methods in criminal investigations too."

A crude version of familial DNA searching was already being used in the United Kingdom to help solve violent crimes, with some success. In one case, the technique had helped solve the murder of a 20-year-old Welsh woman, when, in 2003, 15 years after the crime, a search of the UK National

DNA Database found a partial match between DNA collected at the crime scene and the genetic profile of a teenage boy who had provided a DNA sample when he was convicted of an unrelated offense. As with the Grim Sleeper's son, the boy was too young to have committed the crime, but the information led investigators to the killer, his paternal uncle. Three years later, the same technique helped nab James Lloyd, a prolific rapist in South Yorkshire, England, who had eluded detection for two decades until a familial search brought police to his door.

Increasing the Leads

In 2006, Bieber and David Lazer, then an associate professor of public policy at the Kennedy School (he's now at Northeastern University), and Charles Brenner, then a visiting scholar at the public health school at the University of California, Berkeley, described these cases in a report published in the journal *Science*. What caught the attention of scientists, law enforcement, and the media were the statistics. Using a computer model, the researchers estimated that, by putting familial DNA searching to use in the United States, investigators could increase their leads in criminal cases by 40 percent by searching within a local, state, or national database.

Critics of familial searching say the technique raises a number of troubling issues.

That number has impressed some in law enforcement, among them Rockne Harmon. A retired Alameda County prosecutor and current legal consultant, he was a driving force behind the use of familial DNA searching in California, lobbying state Attorney General Jerry Brown and others for its approval in 2008. "This is just another tool to help us exploit DNA evidence to its fullest potential," he says. "Why shouldn't we take advantage of that?"

Yet critics of familial searching say the technique raises a number of troubling issues. Forty-seven states require that people provide a DNA sample after being convicted of a felony, some require it upon conviction for a misdemeanor, and a growing number of states collect samples from anyone who has even been arrested in connection with a felony crime. The state databases where those samples are compiled are heavily weighted with minorities, notes UCLA law professor Jennifer Mnookin, because those minorities have higher rates of arrests and convictions. (The reasons for those rates are, of course, much debated.) "If we search databases that are already filled with more African-Americans and Latinos than whites, we're going to be more likely to find racial minorities that commit crimes," she explains. "And because the populations contained in the databases aren't race- or class-neutral, it's not a matter of luck if the relatives of those populations are affected."

A Department of Justice survey suggests that 46 percent of jail inmates have another close family member who's also been incarcerated.

While he shares those concerns, Bieber points out that in individual cases, DNA itself "is race blind. We don't know or care whether the owner of that DNA is black, white, or green. Labs are searching every profile in the database regardless of their race or ethnicity." The odds such a search will lead investigators to the relative of a known offender are high: A Department of Justice survey suggests that 46 percent of jail inmates have another close family member who's also been incarcerated.

The Problem of Racial Inequality

Others argue that DNA databases are a reflection, not a cause, of racial inequalities. "If this information is going to be useful for solving a crime, should we not use the data because they're demographically unrepresentative?" asks Lazer. "The real issue that we should be wringing our hands about as a society is why African-Americans have conviction rates around seven times that of whites to begin with."

Another concern about familial DNA searching is that it puts criminals' relatives under genetic surveillance—possibly tracked for life and subjected to police harassment—simply because their close family member, whose DNA is on record, may have committed a crime. "This approach can cast a net of suspicion over entire families, based on nothing more than partial DNA matches," says Larry Tipton, head of the Dedham office for the Massachusetts Committee for Public Counsel Services. "It allows genetics to take precedence over everything else."

The concept "sounds chilling in theory," admits Harmon. "But in reality, it's just not true. In California, the cops aren't even aware of the results of a familial search until scientists have narrowed down the suspects even further."

Familial searching involves computerized comparisons of DNA samples, then a ranking in order of the likelihood that the known offender profile is genetically related to the unknown profile generated from crime scene evidence. In the UK, the technique stops there, with lab workers providing law enforcement with a list of partial matches. By chance alone, unrelated people can have similar genetic material, so it's possible that these matches are meaningless false positives. In the case of James Lloyd, police first pursued the partial matches geographically closest to the crime scenes, literally knocking on doors and interviewing people until they stumbled on a viable suspect.

In California and Colorado, however, familial searching involves an additional layer of lab investigation, in which scientists compare Y chromosome markers to further determine whether the DNA from two samples signals a close male genetic relationship. (Although other techniques can tease out close female relatives, they are rarely used, since most violent offenders are male.) Y chromosome testing can remove unrelated profiles, increasing the odds that the DNA samples belong to, say, a father and son, or to brothers. Unlike in the UK, says Bieber, investigators "won't be knocking on any wrong doors. It almost eliminates the chances of false-positive matches."

> *The court concluded that familial DNA searching may be no more intrusive than a witness identifying a perpetrator from a photo lineup of similar-looking suspects.*

An Unintrusive Technique

In the case of the Grim Sleeper, familial searching with Y-chromosome analysis suggested a male genetic relationship between the DNA found at the crime scene and the partial match in the DNA database. That information allowed investigators to follow up with old-fashioned police work: surveillance of the suspect and DNA tests of the pizza crust. The technique, say experts, is likely to hold up in court. Last month, the US Ninth Circuit Court of Appeals ruled against a defendant who claimed that providing a sample to a DNA database where it would be available for possible future familial searching could violate both his rights and those of his relatives. The court concluded that familial DNA searching may be no more intrusive than a witness identifying a perpetrator from a photo lineup of similar-looking suspects.

Since Bieber and Lazer's study in 2006, just California and Colorado have approved the use of familial DNA searching as an investigative tool, although other states have expressed interest. One of the roadblocks to its use, says Bieber, is a general lack of understanding about the technique and lack of communication between scientific and law enforcement staffs, gaps he and Lazer have worked to bridge through educational lectures and conferences.

Questions about the legality of familial searching has also slowed its acceptance. "Lab workers and law enforcement keep saying, 'We need new legislation to do this,'" says Harmon. But "we didn't change our law in California to allow familial searching. It should be as simple as creating a policy."

There's currently no written policy in Massachusetts to prevent scientists from passing such a clue on to police— but also no policy that allows it.

In 2007, a critical report on the Massachusetts State Police crime lab by the consulting firm Vance recommended that the lab make development of a policy for familial searching a priority. Implementation of the technique would only require submitting a policy to Governor Deval Patrick and getting his approval, but change remains slow. Additional resources, such as special software and scientists trained in this type of DNA analysis, would be necessary, according to Vallaro.

Although the lab has no plans to implement familial searching of its criminal DNA databases, it has begun discussions—what Vallaro calls "the first step"—toward instituting a related approach: case-specific partial matching. Case-specific partial matching relies on the similarities between the DNA of close family members but doesn't involve a search of offender databases. Imagine a case in which a woman is murdered, and blood is left at the crime scene. Investigators ask for voluntary DNA samples from everyone in the household, including the husband, or obtain samples through a search warrant, to look for a complete match or to exclude a person altogether. "A lab worker can examine that DNA and say, 'Nope, the perpetrator isn't the husband,'" Lazer says. But if the evidence is a partial match to the husband's DNA, chances are good that it comes from a close male relative—the husband's brother, for instance.

Legal Issues Need to Be Addressed

There's currently no written policy in Massachusetts to prevent scientists from passing such a clue on to police—but also no policy that allows it. As a result, the practice among State Police crime-lab employees has been not to share partial matches with investigators. Vallaro says he has asked the state's Forensic Science Advisory Board to discuss a possible policy that would allow case-specific partial matching.

Until then, proponents of familial DNA searching and partial matching worry that concerns about public policy and civil liberties may delay implementation of a tool that has the potential not only to catch criminals but also to prevent more victims of violent crime. Meanwhile, Bieber and others say the Grim Sleeper case has set an example of how the technique should be used. "California has done things right from the beginning," says Bieber. "Law enforcement reserved familial searching for violent crimes where other investigative methods had failed, and lab employees made sure that the DNA profile data remained anonymous as long as possible."

Mnookin agrees: "I've generally been pretty impressed by California's policy. I hope that when other jurisdictions follow suit, they'll remember these lessons."

12

DNA Databases Can Help Determine a Person's Identity

Michael Warren

Michael Warren has been writing for the Associated Press for over twenty years. He oversees AP operations in Argentina, Chile, Paraguay, and Uruguay.

After having been abducted as a baby, a 32-year-old Argentinian man finally learned his true identity—thanks to his biological father's efforts to create a large DNA database. DNA samples finally made a reunion possible—a feat otherwise unthinkable— demonstrating the positive influence such databases can have on individuals' lives.

The search is finally over for Abel Madariaga, whose pregnant wife was kidnapped by Argentine security forces 32 years ago.

After decades of doubt and loneliness, of searching faces in the street in hopes they might be related, Madariaga has found his son.

"I never stopped thinking I would find him," the 59-year-old father said, squeezing his son's arm during a packed news conference Tuesday [February 23, 2010].

"For the first time, I know who I was. Who I am," the young man said, still marveling at his new identity: Francisco Madariaga Quintela, a name he only learned last week.

Stolen at Birth

The Grandmothers of the Plaza de Mayo rights group believes about 400 children were stolen at birth from women who were kidnapped and killed as part of the 1976–1983 dictatorship's "dirty war" against political dissidents, which killed as many as 30,000 people.

[Abel Madariaga] has made finding the children of those who disappeared his life's cause.

Madariaga and his wife, Silvia Quintela, were members of the Montoneros, a leftist group targeted for elimination by government death squads. He last saw his wife—a 28-year-old surgeon who treated the poor in a Buenos Aires suburb—being pushed into a Ford Falcon by army officers dressed as civilians as she walked to a train on Jan. 17, 1977.

Madariaga managed to flee into exile to avoid the same fate. Ever since, he has made finding the children of those who disappeared his life's cause.

Returning to a democratic Argentina in 1983, he became the grandmothers group's secretary and first male member. He lobbied the government to create a DNA database and dedicate judicial resources to the effort, and developed strategies for persuading young people with doubts about their identities to come forward and get DNA tests.

All the while, his own son's fate remained a mystery.

As it turned out, Quintela gave birth to the son the couple had planned to name Francisco in July 1977 while imprisoned in one of Argentina's largest and most notorious clandestine torture centers, the Campo de Mayo in suburban Buenos Aires. Surviving prisoners later reported that the newborn was taken from her the next day, and she disappeared shortly thereafter.

Growing up Among Strangers

A military intelligence officer, Victor Alejandro Gallo, brought the baby, his umbilical cord still attached, home to his wife, Ines Susana Colombo. They named him Alejandro Ramiro Gallo and never told him he was adopted. The marriage didn't last—Gallo was a violent man, Francisco Madariaga said—and he never felt like he belonged, looking nothing like his brother and sister.

While the Gallo family fell apart, the younger Madariaga escaped in his own way, twice touring Europe as a professional juggler.

Meanwhile, Gallo was convicted of murdering a couple and their child during a robbery in 1994 and served a 10-year prison term.

Francisco Madariaga's doubts increased, until finally he confronted his adoptive mother. "She broke down and was able to tell me the truth," he recalled, adding that he can't say he blames her. "There was so much violence—physical and mental—and she suffered. She also was a victim."

On Feb. 3 [2010], encouraged by his friends, the young man and Colombo approached the grandmothers group to tell their story. Fearful of Gallo, they rushed to take a blood test the next day, and DNA results arrived last week. Father and son finally met on Friday—the same day Gallo was arrested on suspicion of illegal adoption.

To have your identity is the most beautiful thing there is.

Colombo also has been detained and questioned, according to an attorney for the grandmothers group, Alan Iud. Colombo and Gallo are represented by public defenders who didn't respond to calls after hours Tuesday.

Trembling before the cameras, Abel Madariaga recalled his reunion with his son.

"When he came through the door that night, we recognized each other totally, and the hug that brought us together was spectacular," he said.

Finding His True Identity

Over the years, the grandmothers group has succeeded in identifying 100 children of the disappeared. Madariaga has organized many news conferences announcing such victories. This time, his chest heaved as he presented his own son to the world.

"At times I wondered what the hell I was living for. I had to find a way to continue, thinking about everyday things, hoping for this moment of happiness," the elder Madariaga said. "Hugging him that first time, it was as if I filled a hole in my soul."

Francisco Madariaga stopped smiling only at the mention of the name he was given by the Gallos.

"Never again" will I use this name, he said. "To have your identity is the most beautiful thing there is."

13

DNA Databases Can Help in the Fight Against Animal Cruelty

American Society for the Prevention of Cruelty to Animals (ASPCA)

The ASPCA was the first humane organization in the Western Hemisphere, founded in 1866. Its mission is to provide useful means for the prevention of cruelty to animals in the United States.

To effectively combat dog-fighting, ASPCA has established the first national canine DNA database. Similar to the FBI's human database, Canine CODIS can connect investigations worldwide and will help to cut down on still-profitable businesses that dog-fighting rings are conducting internationally.

The nation's first criminal dog-fighting DNA database has been established by the American Society for the Prevention of Cruelty to Animals (ASPCA), The Humane Society of Missouri (HSMO) and the Louisiana SPCA (LA/SPCA), and will be maintained at the University of California, Davis (UC Davis) Veterinary Genetics Laboratory. Known as the Canine CODIS (Combined DNA Index System), the database is designed to help the criminal justice system investigate and prosecute dog fighting cases and address the growing problem of dog fighting using 21st century technology.

Animal Cruelty and Crime

"Dog fighting is a multi-million dollar criminal enterprise that leads to the cruel treatment and deaths of thousands of dogs nationwide every year," said Tim Rickey, the ASPCA's Senior Director of Field Investigation and Response. "This database is an unprecedented and vital component in the fight against animal cruelty and will allow us to strengthen cases against animal abusers and seek justice for their victims."

This database breaks new ground in supplying . . . evidence for dog fighting investigations.

"This database will connect investigations across the country and internationally, creating multi-jurisdictional collaboration," said Ms. Destreza, who presented on the Canine CODIS at the recent Veterinary Forensics Conference in Orlando, Fla. "It's another tool we can use toward the elimination of dog fighting."

Dr. Merck, who testifies as a forensic veterinary expert for animal cruelty cases around the country, added, "Juries expect forensic science to support the evidence that's presented to them, and animal cruelty cases are no exception. This database breaks new ground in supplying that evidence for dog fighting investigations."

The Canine CODIS contains individual DNA profiles from dogs that have been seized during dog-fighting investigations and from unidentified samples collected at suspected dog-fighting venues. The HSMO provided the 400 original and initial samples of dog DNA collected from dogs that were seized last July [2009] during the nation's largest dog-fighting seizure ever, a multi-state raid led by Mr. Rickey that followed an 18-month investigation by federal and state agencies.

An Important Tool to Fight Animal Abuse

The database is similar to the FBI's human CODIS, a computerized archive that scores DNA profiles from criminal offenders and crime scenes and is used in criminal and missing person investigations. DNA analysis and matching through the database will help law enforcement agencies to identify relationships between dogs, enabling investigators to establish connections between breeders, trainers, and dog-fight operators. Blood collected from dog fighting sites will also be searched against the Canine CODIS database to identify the source.

DNA evidence not only establishes links between owners, breeders, and dog fighting sites, it tells a story.

"The Veterinary Genetics Laboratory has one of the largest sample databases in the world," said Beth Wictum, Director of the Forensics Unit of the Veterinary Genetics Laboratory in UC Davis' School of Veterinary Medicine. "This is important for estimating the rarity of a DNA profile. The Canine CODIS database is unique because it includes many more DNA markers than are normally tested, and that provides greater power when calculating match probability or assigning parentage."

"When these cases come to trial, it's important to make your strongest case," she adds. "DNA evidence not only establishes links between owners, breeders, and dog fighting sites, it tells a story. We can tie blood spatter on pit walls and clothing, or blood trails found outside of the pit, to a specific dog and tell his story for him. We become the voice for those victims."

The Canine CODIS Database

DNA samples from animals have been used in forensics investigations for over 15 years to help solve criminal investigations. In some cases, the animal may be related to the suspect, the victim or the crime scene. In other cases, the animal itself is the victim or perpetrator.

In dog-fighting investigations, the dogs' inner cheeks are swabbed to collect DNA in their saliva at the time they are seized. These swab samples are then submitted to UC Davis Veterinary Genetics Laboratory for DNA testing. Law enforcement agencies also collect DNA at suspected dog-fighting venues in samples of blood, saliva, tissue, bones, teeth, feces and urine. These unidentified DNA samples can be submitted to the laboratory at UC Davis for analysis and archiving in the database.

The ASPCA estimates that there are tens of thousands of people involved in dog fighting in the United States.

When an agency submits a sample to the Veterinary Genetics Laboratory, the DNA is analyzed and the Canine CODIS database is then searched for corresponding DNA profiles. In the event the database search locates a match for the submitted DNA, the lab will notify both the agency that submitted the new sample and the agency that submitted the existing sample. The Canine CODIS database is only available to law enforcement agencies; analysis is part of the cost of testing.

Although there are no official statistics, the ASPCA estimates that there are tens of thousands of people involved in dog fighting in the United States. Dog fighting is a federal crime, as well as a felony offense in all 50 U.S. states.

Organizations to Contact

The editors have compiled the following list of organizations concerned with the issues debated in this book. The descriptions are derived from materials provided by the organizations. All have publications or information available for interested readers. The list was compiled on the date of publication of the present volume; names, addresses, phone and fax numbers, and e-mail and Internet addresses may change. Be aware that many organizations take several weeks or longer to respond to inquiries, so allow as much time as possible.

American Academy of Forensic Sciences (AAFS)
410 North 21st Street, Colorado Springs, CO   80904
(719) 636-1100 • fax: (719) 636-1993
website: www.aafs.org

As a professional society dedicated to the application of science to the law, the AAFS is committed to the promotion of education and the elevation of accuracy, precision, and specificity in the forensic sciences. It does so via the *Journal of Forensic Sciences*, newsletters, its annual scientific meeting, the conduct of seminars and meetings, and the initiation of actions and reactions to various issues of concern.

American Civil Liberties Union (ACLU)
125 Broad St., 18th Fl., New York, NY   10004
(212) 944-0800 • fax: (212) 549-2500
website: www.aclu.org

The ACLU is an organization that works to defend the rights and principles delineated in the Declaration of Independence and the US Constitution. It opposes the censorship of any form of speech, including media depictions of violence. The ACLU publishes the semiannual *Civil Liberties* in addition to policy statements and reports. Its concerns regarding DNA databases focus on privacy and liberty concerns.

American Society of Law, Medicine & Ethics (ASLME)

765 Commonwealth Avenue, Suite 1634, Boston, MA 02215
(617) 262-4990 • fax: (617) 437-7596
e-mail: info@aslme.org
website: www.aslme.org

ASLME is a public research and advocacy organization. It has undertaken a multi-year exploration project of ethical, legal, and social issues surrounding the use of forensic DNA profiling known as the DNA Fingerprinting and Civil Liberties Project. It publishes two quarterly journals, *The Journal of Law, Medicine & Ethics* and *American Journal of Law & Medicine.*

Council for Responsible Genetics (CRG)

5 Upland Road, Suite 3, Cambridge, MA 02140
617 868-0870 • fax: (617) 491-5344
e-mail: crg@gene-watch.org
website: www.councilforresponsiblegenetics.org

Founded in 1983, CRG is a nonprofit, non-governmental organization based in Cambridge, Massachusetts. CRG works through the media and concerned citizens to distribute accurate information and represent the public interest on emerging issues in biotechnology. CRG also publishes a bimonthly magazine, *GeneWatch.*

Department of Justice—DNA Initiative

Office of Justice Programs, Office of Communications
(202) 307-0703
website: www.dna.gov

The DNA Initiative provides funding, training and assistance to guarantee that forensic DNA is used effectively to solve crimes, protect the innocent, and identify missing persons. Its website offers detailed information on the use of DNA evidence, possible risks, and in-depth material on DNA backlogs, false positives, and exonerations.

Federal Bureau of Investigation (FBI)

FBI New York, New York, NY   10278-0004
(212) 384-1000 • fax: (212) 384-4073
e-mail: ny1@ic.fbi.gov
website: www.fbi.gov

The FBI's CODIS Unit manages the Combined DNA Index System (CODIS) and the National DNA Index System (NDIS) and is responsible for developing, providing, and supporting the CODIS Program to federal, state, and local crime laboratories in the United States and selected international law enforcement crime laboratories to foster the exchange and comparison of forensic DNA evidence from violent crime investigations. The CODIS Unit also provides the *Handbook of Forensic Services* to the public online.

Federal Trade Commission (FTC)

600 Pennsylvania Avenue, NW, Washington, DC   20580
(202) 326-2222
website: www.ftc.gov

The FTC deals with issues of the everyday economic life. It is the only federal agency with both consumer protection and competition jurisdiction. The FTC strives to enforce laws and regulations and to advance consumers' interests by sharing its expertise with federal and state legislatures and US and international government agencies. Articles on the issues surrounding DNA databases are available online.

The Innocence Project

40 Worth St., Suite 701, New York, NY   10013
(212) 364-5340
e-mail: info@innocenceproject.org
website: www.innocenceproject.org

The Innocence Project is an advocacy organization that pioneered the use of DNA tests to exonerate wrongfully convicted persons. Under the auspices of law school professors and legal staffs, law students generally take on either "cold cases" or cases in which DNA forensic technology was not available at the time.

National Center for Missing & Exploited Children (NCMEC)
Charles B. Wang International Children's Building
Alexandria, VA   22314-3175
(703) 224-2150 • fax: (703) 224-2122
website: www.ncmec.org

NCMEC assists in finding missing children and supports victims of child abduction and sexual exploitation. The NCMEC website provides articles on how DNA evidence is used to identify missing children.

Bibliography

Books

David Balding	*Weight-of-Evidence for Forensic DNA Profiles.* Hoboken, NJ: John Wiley & Sons, 2006.
Lindell Bromham	*Reading the Story in DNA: A Beginner's Guide to Molecular Evolution.* New York: Oxford University Press, 2008.
John Buckleton, Christopher Triggs, and Simon Walsh	*Forensic DNA Evidence Interpretation.* Boca Raton, FL: CRC Press, 2004.
John Butler	*Forensic DNA Typing: Biology, Technology, and Genetics Behind STR Markers.* Maryland Heights, MO: Academic Press, 2005.
John Butler	*Fundamentals of Forensic DNA Typing.* Maryland Heights, MO: Academic Press, 2009.
Greg Cooper and Mike King	*Cold Case Methodology.* San Clemente, CA: LawTech, 2005.
Sorin Draghici	*Bioinformatics Databases: Design, Implementation, and Usage.* Boca Raton, FL: CRC Press, 2010.
Wing Kam Fung and Yue-Qing Hu	*Statistical DNA Forensics: Theory, Methods and Computation.* Hoboken, NJ: John Wiley & Sons, 2008.

Deborah Gage   *FBI: Cold Case Files.* Memphis, TN:
                            Baseline, 2005.

William   *An Introduction to Forensic Genetics.*
Goodwin, Adrian   Hoboken, NJ: John Wiley and Sons,
Linacre, and Sibte   2011.
Hadi

Richard   *Genetic Suspects: Global Governance*
Hindmarsh and   *of Forensic DNA.* New York:
Barbara Prainsack   Cambridge University Press: 2010.

Stacy Horn   *The Restless Sleep: Inside New York*
                            City's Cold Case Squad. New York:
                            Penguin, 2005.

Lawrence   *DNA: Forensic and Legal Applications.*
Kobilinsky,   Hoboken NJ: Wiley-Interscience,
Thomas Liotti,   2004.
and Jamel
Oeser-Sweat

Sheldon Krimsky   *Genetic Justice: DNA Data Banks,*
and Tania   *Criminal Investigations, and Civil*
Simoncelli   *Liberties.* New York: Columbia
                            University Press, 2010.

David Lazer, ed.   *DNA and the Criminal Justice System:*
                            The Technology of Justice (Basic
                            Bioethics). Boston: MIT Press, 2004.

Richard Li   *Forensic Biology: Identification and*
                            DNA Analysis of Biological Evidence.
                            Boca Raton, FL: CRC, 2008.

Michael Lynch, Simon A. Cole, Ruth McNally, and Kathleen Jordan	*Truth Machine: The Contentious History of DNA Fingerprinting.* Chicago: University of Chicago Press, 2009.
Mustafa Man, Julaily Aida Jusoh, and Md. Yazid Mohd Saman	*Bio-Informatics: Formal Specification for DNA Database System.* Saarbrücken, Germany: LAP LAMBERT Academic Publishing, 2011.
Kenneth Rainis	*Blood and DNA Evidence: Crime-Solving Science Experiments.* Berkeley Heights, NJ: Enslow, 2007.
Gina Smith	*The Genomics Age: How DNA Technology Is Transforming the Way We Live and Who We Are.* New York: AMACOM, 2005.
Charles Swanson, Neil Chamelin, Leonard Territo, and Robert Taylor	*Criminal Investigation.* New York: McGraw-Hill, 2006.
Richard Walton	*Cold Case Homicides: Practical Investigative Techniques.* Boca Raton, FL: CRC Press, 2006.
Roger Wilkes, ed.	*The Mammoth Book of Unsolved Crime: The Biggest and Best Collection of Unsolved Murder and Mystery Cases,* New York: Carroll & Graf, 2005.

Periodicals

Wilton Alston	"Building a DNA Database," *The New American*, Vol. 24, June 9, 2008.
Deborah Baskin and Ira Sommers	"Crime-show-viewing Habits and Public Attitudes toward Forensic Evidence: The "CSI Effect" Revisited," *Justice System Journal*, Vol. 31, 2010.
David Caudill	"Genetic Witness: Science, Law, and Controversy in the Making of DNA Profiling," *Journal of Criminal Law and Criminology*, Vol. 98, Winter 2008.
Elizabeth M. Collins	"Shining Light on Battlefield Forensics," *Soldiers*, Vol. 65, June 2010.
The Daily Mail (London)	"Should We Have a National DNA Database?" February 29, 2008.
The Daily Mail (London)	"Should We Keep the Innocent on DNA Database?" May 12, 2009.
Charles Davis, Suzanne Ogilby, and Ramona Farrell	"Survival of the Analytically Fit: The DNA of an Effective Forensic Accountant," *Journal of Accountancy*, Vol. 210, August 2010.
Joe Donohue	"Untapped Potential: Funds Shortages Prevent Extensive Use of Forensic DNA," *The Forensic Examiner*, Vol. 16, Summer 2007.

Larry A.
Hammond
"1 in 10 of Us on DNA Database; Police Defend Using Samples," *Evening Chronicle* (Newcastle, England), October 29, 2008.

Larry A.
Hammond
"The Failure of Forensic Science Reform in Arizona," *Judicature*, Vol. 93, No. 6, May–June 2010.

Sarah Hammond
"The DNA Factor: Lawmakers Are Expanding the Use of Forensic Technology to Battle Crime," *State Legislatures*, Vol. 36, June 2010.

Doug Hanson
"DNA Evidence: A Powerful Tool," *Law & Order*, Vol. 55, April 2007.

Leonard Johns,
Gerard Downes,
and Camille
Bibles
"FBI to Expand DNA Database," *Information Management Journal*, Vol. 43, July 2009.

Leonard Johns,
Gerard Downes,
and Camille
Bibles
"Resurrecting Cold Case Serial Homicide Investigations," *FBI Law Enforcement Bulletin*, August 2005.

Donna Lyons
"Capturing DNA's Crime Fighting Potential," *State Legislatures*, Vol. 32, March 2006.

Josh P. Roberts
"Amplifying Trouble," *The Scientist*, Vol. 22, April 2008.

Stacy St. Clair
"How Forensics Found the DNA," *Daily Herald* (Arlington Heights, IL), April 17, 2007.

Michael J. Saks   "The Past and Future of Forensic Science and the Courts," *Judicature*, Vol. 93, 2009.

Melissa Solomon   "Righting Old Wrongs," *Fed Tech Magazine*, November 2006.

Sonia M. Suter   "All in the Family: Privacy and DNA Familial Searching," *Harvard Journal of Law & Technology*, Vol. 23, No. 2, Spring 2010.

Peter Wilby   "The Innocent Could Be Taken off DNA Database; Court Rules Holding Details Is a Breach of People's Human Rights," *Western Mail* (Cardiff, Wales), December 5, 2008.

Peter Wilby   "What They Know about Us . . . Your Postcode Reveals More Than Your DNA Can," *New Statesman*, Vol. 136, September 17, 2007.

Joseph Yost and Tod Burke   "Veterinary Forensics: Animals Curtailing Crime," *FBI Law Enforcement Bulletin*, Vol. 76, October 2007.

Index